ACKNOWLEDGEMENTS

I thank the Lord for all He has done in establishing the CHIPS ministry and in helping me to write this book. The list of people whom I would like to thank seems endless.

First, to my Mom and Dad, thank you for your faithfulness in loving one another and your children; you gave me an incredible treasury of love to share. To my wife Susan, who is a woman of integrity, without guile, thank you for staying flexible. To my loving children, thank you for the honor you so freely give to me.

To all the mentors, friends, and loved ones who have given from their hearts to help train this "kid from the Bronx," thank you.

To Elim Fellowship, especially Mike Cavanaugh, I want to express my gratitude for allowing me to share the integrity of the Father-heart and for allowing me many years of opportunity to serve the body of Christ.

Thanks also to the church family at North Chili Community Church in Rochester, New York, for allowing me the time to complete this project; to Pastors Carl Jenks and David Meyer whose encouragement and support challenged me to stay on track; to my administrator, Nancy Nasso for sharing her exceptional administrative gifts and taking charge so that I could find the time to write. Special thanks to our dear friends and neighbors, Jim and Karen Fenton, for editing and assisting in the completion of this project, and to the church family at New Covenant Community Church in Audubon, New Jersey, especially to Wendy McDermott for her faithful help and prompting to get the job done.

I am also grateful to all the family of God who so wonderfully touched Susan's heart and mine and allowed us to minister in the "land down under," especially Pastors Alan Meyer in Melbourne and Paul O'Sullivan in Northern Beaches, Sydney, Australia.

DEDICATION

*This book is dedicated
to the memory of my son, James Christian,
our first-born, who was a bright light
while here for sixteen years.
He remains an inspiration
to all who knew him.
His life and death have taken me
to a new level in understanding
the Father heart of God.*

CONTENTS

FORWARD

In our day of attempts to "look good" and to create good impressions by people who are nearly plastic, it is my personal joy to commend to you Tony's book. Tony is real, his family is real, and the issues with which he deals in the life of the single-parent family are also very real. It is important that we take Tony's testimony seriously because it describes the birth of his vision. It is a heart burden which he has attempted to put on paper.

One sense that came over me as I sought to absorb the vision he describes was: "It seems to me that Tony is presenting a message that seems fairly heavy." Almost immediately upon beginning to read this book, I was jolted awake by the fact that the very issues that he seeks to address are themselves heavy. Those, like me, who would experience the actual weight of what he wants to communicate need to come to grips with the dreadful consequence of the assault on the family.

Someone once said, "My beautiful theories were murdered by a gang of ugly facts." The modern theories suggesting that it is acceptable for people to say "Divorce is my privilege. I do not want to be inconvenienced. Parental responsibilities are too demanding," are now being "murdered by the ugly facts of life." This book deals, in brutal honesty, with the facts of single-family parenting, which many must face on a continual basis. Few issues remain as critical, unacknowledged, and unattended to as this one. Parental strife is *pandemic*, which means that it is one step *beyond* epidemic. If you are even *thinking* that my statement is exaggerated or alarmist, I invite you to examine the list of the hidden costs of divorce that are given in Chapter 1.

Allow me along with the author, to appeal to pastors and church leaders to examine these issues in light of providing clearer answers and regular support for the growing number of women and men who feel they are being marginalized or even disenfranchised by the church of the Lord Jesus. They really think that the church does not care or that we do not know the fear and loneliness that they face. They hear the preaching as designed for those who are "normal" families. Tony, like the New Testament itself, appeals to us to learn to love those who are different, those who may be alienated, and those who may have failed in the past.

We want to know the answers Tony gives to the problems we face. I challenge the church, as Tony does, not to *fail to take the medicine.* As Tony explains in Chapter 3, *we, too, may need a roll of quarters.*

— *Bob Mumford*

SPECIAL WORD

With tear-stained faces lining the altar and filling the front of the church we closed the service, vividly aware that we had just heard from God. It was the spring of 1989. Our guest speaker for that Sunday morning service had been Tony Martorana. His message had been a wake-up call to the church regarding the plight of single parents and their children, a segment of the population even within the church that was "slipping through the cracks." There was hardly a dry eye in the church! I particularly remember Ralph, one of our young dads, standing at the altar with tears streaming down his face. When Tony left that day we knew that we had heard from God, but we didn't know exactly how to proceed. Fortunately for us, the Lord intended to answer the heart cry of that morning in a very dramatic and life changing way. Two years later Tony became part of our pastoral team, and we became the home base for CHIPS.

Six years later we have seen the ministry blossom into a marvelous work of the Father, which has been used to touch hundreds and hundreds of lives literally around the world. We have seen multitudes of single parents and their children receive healing, hope and a "home." In the process we have discovered just how much our Father loves these wounded ones and how much joy he delights to give to them, and to those who minister to them. Our hearts have been permanently changed in the process. As you read these pages, yours will be too.

Tony is a man whose heart burns with a word from God. You cannot be near him for any length of time and not be touched by his revelation of the heart of the Father. He is a man of God with a love for the family of God, and especially for those who have been attacked and damaged by the enemy of their souls. Tony ministers out of a heart of compassion, forged in the furnace of pain and trial— his own and others'. He has a two-fold message to all who read this book. To those who are the victims, single parents and their children, he extends a message of hope. To the church, Tony shares the heart cry of the Father to no longer neglect this essential aspect of ministry and care. God cares for all His children. He has a way for us to do the same. Ministry to single parents and their children is one that is filled with challenge and great reward.

Whether you are a single parent, a single-parent child, or a Christian desiring to know more about this vital area of ministry, this book is for you. I am confident that as you read it you will discover more of the Father's Heart than you have known before. Happy reading and discovering!

Carl Jenks
Pastor,
North Chili Community Church
Rochester, New York

Information on CHIPS

CHIPS HOME OFFICE

C.H.I.P.S.
New Covenant Community Church
255 Edgewood Avenue
Audubon, NJ 08106
Phone: (609) 546-0344
Fax: (609) 546-6498

CHIPS HOST CHURCHES/USA

Believer's Chapel, 7912 Thompson Road, Cicero, NY 13039;
Phone: (315) 699-4414; Fax: (315) 699-1370

Full Gospel Christian Center, 415 Old Town Rd.,
Port Jefferson Station, NY 11776; Phone: (516) 928-6100;
Fax: (516) 928-6291

New Covanent Community Church (C.H.I.P.S. National
Headquarters), 255 Edgewood Avenue, Audubon, NJ 08106;
Phone: (609) 546-0344; Fax (609) 546-6498

North Chili Community Church, 3355 Union St.,
P.O. Box 279, N. Chili, NY 14514; Phone: (716) 594-2010;
Fax: (716) 594-0191

CHIPS HOST CHURCHES/AUSTRALIA

Mt. Evelyn Christian Fellowship, 89 Monbulk Road, Mt. Evelyn, Australia 3796; Phone: (03) 9736-2323; Fax: (Australia): 03 9736 1344; Fax (Int'l): 61 3 9736 1344

Northern Beaches Christian Centre, Echunga Road, P.O. Box 230, Terrey Hills, Australia 2084; Phone: (30) 9450-1706; Fax: 9450-1478

CHIPS SENSITIVE CHURCHES AND SPONSORS

Bethlehem Assembly of God, 12 E. Fair View Ave., Valley Stream, PA 11580; Phone: (516) 561-6150

Bethesda Christian Church, 14000 Metropolitan Parkway, Sterling Heights, Michigan 48312 -3402; Phone: (810) 264 -2300

Christ Community Church, 1201 Slate Hill Rd., Camp Hill, PA 17011; Phone: (717) 761-2933; Fax: (717)761-4236

Church of Love Faith Center, 100 Brooks Ave., Rochester, NY 14619; Phone: (716) 328-5022

Creative Word Ministries, P.O. Box 551, Lima, NY 14485; Phone: (716) 582-2130, Fax: (716) 582-1251

Elim Gospel Church, 7245 College, Lima, NY 14485; Phone: (716) 624-5560

Family Worship Center, 1201 Parade St., Erie, PA 16503; Phone: (814) 455-7730, Fax: (814) 456-5547

Lifechangers, PO Box 98088, Raleigh, NC; Phone: (919) 676-3500, (800) 521-5676

New Jerusalem Community Church, 890 N. Goodman St., Rochester, NY 14609; Phone: (716) 288-0030

New Life Assembly of God, PO Box 638, 424 Main St., Ogdensburg, NY 13669; Phone: (315) 393-0470

Oakland Christian Church, 5100 N. Adams Rd., Oakland Township, MI 48306; Phone: (248) 650-8100

Shepherd's Heart Christian Fellowship, 1301 Long Pond Rd., Rochester, NY 14626; Phone: (716) 225-4090

Zion Fellowship, 236 Gorham St., Canandaigua, NY 14424; Phone: (716) 394-5482

Chapter One

SATAN'S ATTACK ON THE FAMILY

Single-parent ministry is on the heart of our heavenly Father, and now more than ever its issues must be addressed by the family of God. This book is written to help educate, equip, and encourage the single-parent family and to help equip the church for the challenge of supporting single-parent families.

People can end up as single parents by way of various paths — by becoming divorced, by being abandoned, by becoming a parent out of wedlock, or by the death of a spouse — but the challenges of parenting alone and dealing with the issues of relationships that have been injured or cut off are similar regardless of the cause of the separation. Some comments I've written may seem directed to particular segments of the single parent population; nevertheless, all readers can glean truth from the principles and examples presented and apply them to their individual situation.

It is with great hope that I pen this book. My hope is that Jesus Christ will illuminate hearts and minds through His Holy Spirit so that we might grab hold of His truth for the sake of every individual caught in a marriage that has been attacked by Satan. When we become involved in single-parent family ministry, there is a sense that we are moving into an active warzone laden with casualties. Whether you are entering the battle to release those held in captivity or you wish to be set free yourself, this book offers both practical and spiritual insight.

Many have been blinded by the suddenness of the enemy's ambush. Many of those wounded in the family have been taken captive as prisoners of war. It is obvious that a Satanic attack against marriage is in full force. Why is this happening? What is Satan's ultimate objective? What does the enemy hope to accomplish in attacking the marital institution? The people affected by divorce are taken captive by fear, anger, hatred, rejection, and vengeance, with the ultimate objective being to turn their hearts from God. This war for the soul is not a recent phenomenon. It has been waged since the garden of Eden, and one of the main battlegrounds for the soul has been within family relationships.

The home can be fractured by any member, including the children. The pressures that exist in the American home today are evenly distributed among all its members. For a marriage not solidly rooted and grounded in Christ, the least bit of pressure can be enough to cause the husband-wife relationship to fracture. Today, like never before, the enemy has twisted and deceived our children to the point that even they are being used in the demise of a family: children are suing parents over methods of discipline; drugs and sexual problems are affecting our youth in epidemic proportion; and rebellion and violence are tearing at the fiber of the American home. I have heard others in ministry say that the blame for the divorce or separation cannot be placed on the children, and I agree that the ultimate fault is in the parent's relationship. But I *have* seen children who were guilty of making the home life miserable. Children can open the way for the enemy to gain a foothold so that he can then attack the relationship between the parents. Children must be held accountable, confronted in mercy and truth, and brought to a place of repentance.

The Bible calls Satan the "adversary" of our soul (I Peter 5:8). Whenever Satan undertakes a battle or a war, you can be sure that his ambition is to capture and destroy souls. In the attack on the family, his objective is the same. He wants to wound the heart of each family member. He is looking to rob individuals of life and hope because in such a desperate condition, they are vulnerable and susceptible to his ways. He wants to get individuals in his grip, turned from a loving relationship with God the Father. But the Lord is not willing for any to perish. He does not want His people taken captive, and He is not going to sit around and watch while His children are kidnapped. As the institution of marriage crumbles, the precious lives caught in the heat of the battle are under intense pressure to turn from God's love. Surely, now is a crucial time to strengthen every marriage in the church, for the battle is not only in the world; the battle is also in God's house, among God's people.

Marriage is the ultimate arena for two people to love and grow in God. No other relationship can keep two people committed to each other in perfect harmony, expressing Christ's love for His Church, spiritually, mentally, and physically. In a good marriage relationship, the fire that burns and sanctifies is red hot. Working through difficulties, dying to self, seeking God's will and walking in it is more intense than the divorce fire. Marriage definitely has a greater degree of Christ-building potential than divorce. It puts you in a microwave experience; there are no flames, you but cook from within.

I pray that any troubled marriage that has any sign of hope or life be reconciled. Signs of life such as a spouse's repentance, willingness to undergo counseling, or openness to mediation can be used by the Lord to restore the relationship. Wherever there is a spark of life, blow on it by putting your energies into reconciliation. Seek godly insight from those respected in the Christian community. Divorce hurts terribly, and that is why God hates the sin that causes divorce. It always winds up hurting someone, if not everyone involved, sometimes for generations. Do whatever it takes to make your marriage work in whatever way the Lord is showing you to see if reconciliation is possible. Get counsel from a pastor or Christian counselor that is wise and who is willing to walk with both of you through the process. Listen, obey, and pray. There are many ministries that can help and have great gifts that will help you and your spouse as you work through your problems. Reach out to them.

As much as I want to see marriages remain whole, I realize that in the eyes of the Lord, marriage is not the ultimate purpose for our being born. The relationship between a husband and a wife, or between a child and a parent, can be precious. God certainly sees marriage as very important. Our Lord, however, explained how much more important our relationship is with Him than any earthly, natural, human relationship. He said in Matthew 10:37 that anybody who puts another person ahead of the Lord is "not worthy" of Him. It's inappropriate for people to worship their mates, their children or their parents and it's just as wrong to worship any human institution, even marriage. I love my wife and children, but I adore Jesus Christ. During my life I've seen too many people live their lives for family, adoring a husband or a wife or children, and failing to surrender to our Lord and Savior. A happy marriage truly is a wonderful goal. Yet our purpose in being born, according to Romans 8:28-29, is to be transformed and conformed into the image of the Beloved. Our ticket into heaven is not dependent upon how long we have been married, but upon what we have done with the Spirit of the Lord Jesus Christ in our lifetime. Imagine the following conversation in heaven:

> **"Fifty, Sir," responds a pious man.**
> **"Enter," Christ tells him joyously. "Strike up the heavenly band."**
> **Then Christ turns to the next in line, a woman who is holding her hands before her face. He asks, "How many years have you been married?"**
> **"Fifteen, but then I got a divorce," she responds, shrinking from the light.**
> **"Depart from me," Christ tells her. "This place is only for those whose families and marriages have remained intact — heaven is a sort of family theme park."**

But that's not the way it will be. The Lord will say to those who have never submitted to his will:

"You have been married for fifty years, but you never bowed your knee to my lordship. You never once thanked me for your wife, who submitted to all of your bizarre behaviors. You never once shared my Son, Jesus, with the children I gave you. Depart from me; I know you were married for fifty years, but I don't know you."

Then He will turn to the one who suffered and yet submitted to His lordship:

"Fifteen years, and divorced. I remember the day you cried out to Me, 'Lord, please help me. What am I to do with the children? How are we to make it?' It was at that moment you called Me into your life, and every step of the way you allowed Me to lead you. My dear child, enter in."

My heart desires to reconcile sinners to the lordship of Jesus Christ. Our heavenly Father wants to preserve every marriage and to see the commitment made by every couple honored, but His ultimate passion is to save every soul and bring each one to Himself. This is His desire no matter what life brings their way. In the church, a higher standard of integrity in relationships than we currently have witnessed must be raised regarding commitment in marriage, but ultimately, if a marriage fails, the souls must still be faithful to the lordship of Christ. The breakup of a marriage is not the unpardonable sin. It is not the occasion for those caught in the calamity to run from

God but rather to run *to* Him. Today, our heavenly Father is raising up the most powerful force on the earth, His church, His body, in order to gather His wounded children together with great compassion and to set free those taken captive, as the Lord says in Isaiah 54: 6-7:

> *"For the Lord has called you,*
> *Like a wife forsaken and grieved in spirit,*
> *Even like a wife of one's youth when she is rejected,"*
> *says your God.*
> *"For a brief moment I forsook you,*
> *But with great compassion I will gather you."*

IDEAL VS. REAL: THE WORLD'S VIEW OF SINGLE-PARENT FAMILIES

The secular world pushes the notion that single-parent families are acceptable and even desirable. Through television and movies, Hollywood portrays the life of the single-parent family as something to behold, even something attractive: *Full House, Kate and Allie, Who's the Boss?, Blossom, Hogan's Place, Grace Under Fire, Scarecrow and Mrs. King,* and *Two Dads,* to mention a few. In these programs, all the family's problems can be solved in 30 minutes between commercials. Movies such as *Mrs. Doubtfire, Three Men and A Baby,* and *One Fine Day* present a false impression of what life in single-parent families is like. Never do you see the single parents hitting the floor on their knees and crying out, "Oh, God, I can't do it on my own!" Never do you see them crying out to a pastor, "Please, give me counsel! I'm totally losing it!"

The shows make single parenting seem all so simple. "Don't worry. Be happy. Everything's going

to be okay. Hire a housekeeper like Tony Danza on
Who's the Boss. I'm sure you can afford one. The problems will just melt away. The kids will just bounce
back. Just give us 30 minutes with a good
scriptwriter, and everything will be all patched up!"
As you and I know, the problems are not so easily
solved. That is not how life is.

THE REAL STORY

Isolation is what single parents often experience. They feel that they are alone with their problems, and nobody else really shares their hurts. Likewise, their children believe they're the only ones with
the problems of single-parent families. In one sense,
I wish that they were right because there would be
only a few people in this situation. Unfortunately,
that is not the case. Although they feel isolated emotionally and socially, they are not in the least isolated
in a numerical sense.

The rise in divorce as well as an increase in
the age at which people are getting married for the
first time are two of the major factors contributing to
the growing proportion of children in one-parent living situations. At present, it is estimated that close
to 30% of all households in America are headed by
single-parents. There were 10.5 million single-parent
families in 1992. According to *The Leading Health Indi-
cators of the American Family in the 90's* by Glenn Stanton
and Christine Yocum, the fastest growing marital-sta-
tus category is divorced persons. The number of currently divorced adults quadrupled from 4.3 million in
1970 to 17.4 million in 1994. According to *Facts
about Single Parent Families* by Parents without Partners,
a nationwide support group for single parents, of the

7 million single parent households that are headed by women with children under the age of 18, 58% are white, 33% are African American, 2% are Asian, and 6% are other racial and ethnic groups. The U.S. Census Bureau predicted in 1987 that by the year 2000, 19 million families would be added to the U.S. population and that only 3 out of 10 would be two-parent families. Thus by the turn of the century there were expected to be almost 13 million families in the single-parent category who were not in that category in 1987.

And it's not just the numbers of people involved in divorce that are staggering. In *Economic Consequences of Marital Dissolution*, sociologist Atlee Stroup and economist Gene Pollock discuss the aftereffects of divorce. They conclude that the average white female experiences a 22% loss in income and the average white male experiences a 10% income loss after divorce due to increased day care expenses, decreased overtime income, and other factors. These losses are considerably higher in the African American population. There are health consequences, as well. Divorced men have nearly a 49% greater chance of dying from heart disease, a 41% greater chance of dying from a stroke, and a 43% greater chance of dying from respiratory cancer than their married counterparts. Divorced men also have a 30% higher suicide rate than married men. In fact according to many researchers, the strongest predictor of stress-related physical and emotional disease is marital disruption.

WHAT ABOUT CHILDREN IN THIS TREND?

Children under the age of eighteen are considerably more likely to be living with only one parent today than two decades ago. In 1994, 27% of all the children in the United States were living in single-parent homes. 25% of white children, and 57% of black children live in a single-parent home. The U.S. Census Bureau has projected that three out of every five children currently under the age of 18 will end up living with only one of their parents because of divorce. 38% of all children live without their biological father. 50% of children with separated parents see their fathers less than once a month. Girls growing up fatherless are two and a half times more likely to have a child out of wedlock than girls who grow up with their fathers present. 70% of the juveniles in state reform institutions grew up without one of their parents, usually without a father.

81% of single-parent households are headed by women, and the majority of custodial parents are women. These facts are reflected at CHIPS conferences where the vast majority of participants are women. According to Parents Without Partners, among women, the largest single-parent group is divorced mothers, accounting for 37%. Next are the mothers who have never been married (33%), followed by mothers who are separated (17%), and widowed (7%).

The fastest-growing of these groups of mother-led households is the never-married mothers, which has multiplied 8.9 times since 1970. In that year there were 248,000 never-married mothers in America. Today there are over 2.2 million. 70% of children born out of wedlock do not have a legally designated father.

A research study done by the National Institute of Mental Health shows that children of divorce display behaviors such as the following:

Severe impairment of scholastic and
social adjustments
Disturbance of sleep and eating patterns
Feelings of despair, helplessness, hopelessness
Slow responsiveness in conversation
Occasional suicidal ideas and threats
Sad affect (unhappy face)
Withdrawal
Periods of agitation
Aggressive behavior
Psychosomatic illness
Sexual promiscuity

These behaviors are the products of the
divorce and parental strife, but they are also the
result of the enemy's using the divorce as a means to
go on the attack.

GOD HEALS THE BROKEN HEARTED

Ministry to thousands of single parents has provided me with valuable insights into the specific problems
that single parents and their children face. The only effective answers to these problems find their foundation in
God's Word. By that I do not refer to some sort of "pie in
the sky" answers. Rather, I mean nitty-gritty, gut-level,
practical answers that give single parents potential for
success as they align themselves with God's revealed
will.

God has used me in ministry to single-parent families in spite of the fact that I came from a traditional two-
parent family. Additionally, for more than 25 years, I
have enjoyed a very healthy and happy marriage to my
wife, Susan. We have had four children. Yet, I've been
in some form of ministry to single parents since 1981. I

11

have often wondered "why me?" Billy Graham has described people like me. He speaks of us as "a turtle on a fence post," pointing out that when you see a turtle on a fence post you know that someone else put it there because it couldn't have gotten up by itself. My sensitivity to those who suffer the agonies of a fractured home life comes, not from a shared experience, but from a God-given vision. I didn't get there on my own.

Years ago, when I began to respond to the burden of the Father's heart, I'd say to myself, "I don't understand people who are divorced. My parents were happily married. My grandparents were married for fifty-five years. Something must be wrong with those people. Someone else can take care of them." But God said, "I didn't call you to minister just to people you are used to — nice, whole, Italian-American families! I called you to minister to *my* family — including single parents and their wounded children. You don't know how? Then get on your knees before me, and I'll open your heart!" I did. He answered, and CHIPS, *Christ's Helpers in Parental Strife*, was born (see details in Chapter 2).

This ministry is effective, not because of a natural, first-hand experience in these matters, but because of God's love for the individuals who are the products of single-parent homes — a love that He has placed supernaturally in my heart. I believe He has given me more than a love for the broken-hearted; I believe He has sensitized my heart and birthed a vision to be shared with them — a vision that will bring healing to them and will restore them to living effectively for the sake of His kingdom! The single parents have not been put on the shelf. No, they are not second-class citizens in the kingdom of God. God has a special calling for them, and I am anxious to help them find it. Let's begin!

Chapter Two

THE BIRTH OF A VISION

How does anyone get started in ministry, and more specifically, in single-parent ministry? A single parent wrote to me saying, "I know why God called you, Tony, to single-parent families even though you have no personal experience with divorce — to show wounded families that 'perfectly ordinary people' in the body of Christ can understand. Praise God for your work." I never thought I would be doing this kind of ministry. God's ways are so far beyond mine.

Every individual whom God calls He takes the time to train and prepare. The person He chooses to use will be fired and tested beforehand. However, many an individual has cracked under the pressure of ministry after somehow managing to by-pass the preparation that God set up because it was too painful to go through. But if we let Him, God will work on the character issues and use the material in His hands to form a vessel through which His power

13

can flow. God spent twenty years molding and refining me for this ministry.

GOD'S FIRST CALL

When God calls us to a ministry — any ministry — the preparation begins in our childhood. He may use blessing or adversity to prepare us for the way He will use us in the future. In my case He blessed me with a wealth of godly influence from my early childhood throughout my teen years. My parents, especially my dad, encouraged me to love God and people by demonstrating these behaviors himself. As an active member in the Roman Catholic church, I was exposed to wonderful role models of priests, nuns, and brothers. God connected me with those who had a specific calling to minister to children. Their tenderness, openness, and affection were models of love toward all children. They were used as catalysts in my life, so much so that I thought about devoting my life to full-time service as a brother in the church. This was squelched by my parents who convinced me that I really wanted to get married.

God will develop us for ministry during times of personal trial. Most Christians realize that people respond in one of two ways when we suffer or someone of influence in our lives suffers: we either mature and become more Christlike moving toward what God has created us to be, or we move further from Christlikeness. We turn away from God and His ways when we listen to man, and take the word of man to heart instead of the Word of God. Instead of hearing God's Word we can become charmed and turn away from His will. His plan is often stored in the back of our minds. We may think at times it's completely forgotten, but it is there. Even though I knew God's call at an early age, I became distracted and chose the world for nearly a decade.

During a time of adversity I turned away from God's will. My father became ill with Parkinson's disease during my first year of college. I wanted to make finances easier for the family, so I decided to join the army to provide some income for my education through the G.I. bill. My dad said, "Well, son, the army's going to make you a man." Instead of realizing that I had been well on the way to manhood by way of character development for eighteen years, I took a detour that lasted nine years. During my time in the service, I fell into the trap of the worldly soldier's mindset: "a real man goes on weekend pass, gets drunk, fights, and finds a woman." Whatever I thought it took to become a man, I did. I became a follower of the world's way, learning from the flesh and the devil.

In 1966, I was honorably discharged from the military. Shortly after my discharge I returned to Iona college, now supported by the G.I. bill. By this time, my head and heart were completely messed up. God was out the window, and I sought to show everyone my new-found manhood. I hung out with young Mafia-type tough guys of the Bronx. It was at this time that something happened that increased the darkness I was in. I loved to sing and would sing "Doo-wop" on the street corners with whatever guys were interested in harmonizing at the moment.

One night as a large group of us went to a nightclub, they jokingly asked the house band to invite "Tony Star" up to sing. I looked around expecting to see someone else stand up, only to realize it was me that they were talking about. I never backed down from a challenge, so I went up to the stage and sang. Because of the large group of guys and girls in the club who knew me, the response to my song sounded like I *was* a star. Not realizing the audience was rigged, the nightclub owner came to me and wanted to hire me. He asked me to sing on Saturday nights. I couldn't believe it, but I said, "Yes." Suddenly, girls, girls, girls came my way without me seeking them, and I quickly became lost in the world of show business.

I got hooked on performing and became very popular as a nightclub singer in the Bronx. I was soon picked up by a management firm from New York City and found my face in *16 Magazine*, a nationwide teen monthly. I had a fan club, and kids were attracted to me for all the wrong reasons, as if I were some kind of a hero. My career in show business quickly became another experience forcing me to learn the ropes and follow the leader in a new environment. Drugs, alcohol, and women were the mainstays of the night life. Yet, with all the success and the pleasures of the world, inside I was very lonely and empty. I didn't like who I had become.

In 1972 as I was preparing to join a new band called The Lemon Tree in Ft. Lauderdale, Florida, God touched my life. On a beautiful sun-filled Florida day, I slithered like a snake out of my motel to pick up a girl on the beach in order to captivate her and take her back to my room. I found a young lady walking on the beach who was beautiful, but she was different. She didn't fall for any of my New York City lines. I pursued her down the beach. Finally, she turned to me and said boldly, "Tony, why don't you slow your life down, and let Jesus Christ lead you to some good friends; you need some good friends."

Immediately, as if I had been stunned by a lighting bolt, I, "Mr. Cool," was speechless. Finally, I said to her, "Could you help me?" She brought me back to a group of young people who had Bibles and guitars. It was as if I had walked into the fullness of light from the world of darkness. I said to myself, "Where did these people come from?" I had never seen such a love for God so outwardly and wonderfully expressed by people who were not members of the clergy. I began spending a lot of time with this group of Christians. Within a matter of weeks, I moved out of the motel and went to live in a Christian home. Jesus Christ became more than religion to me; He became my personal Savior.

I was baptized in the ocean in the cool of night, and I have been wonderfully changed ever since. Excitedly I called home to tell my family about my new found love for God. They didn't understand. Due to my incredibly cunning disguise as the entertainer, my family did not realize the depth of sin I had fallen into. Now they thought I had flipped out, but I told them I had flipped *in*; I *had been* flipped out before. Sin is so deceitful.

Finally I had come to grips with the error of my ways, and I was so happy; I began growing in an understanding of God. The Holy Bible became a living Word, with real applications for my life. After a month I was introduced to the wonderful teaching of Bob Mumford, who was in town speaking. I laughed and cried as I listened to him, and God deposited some powerful seeds in me that I continually benefit from even today. Today, it is wonderful to consider that Brother Bob Mumford is still a father in the faith to me, as well as a CHIPS supporter.

What about my religion? I thought about the years I spent in Catholicism. I had never heard anything about salvation. The relationship with Jesus that these young people in Florida had was so personal and alive. I wondered if I could continue my walk at home. I left Ft. Lauderdale with a copy of *The Living Bible*, a living faith with a fresh hope for life, and a determination to find God at home. My parents had moved from the Bronx to my brother's home in Mahopac, New York. The first Sunday back I went to church. I was thrilled to find a spirit-filled Franciscan priest. Meeting Father Charlie was glorious. He had experienced a wonderful outpouring of the Holy Spirit. I didn't know it at the time, but I was in the middle of the Charismatic renewal in the Catholic Church. Charlie taught me much, and as I worked with him I fell head over heels in love with Jesus, and I rediscovered the love I had for working with youth.

One of the many practical experiences I had was working in a camp in the Pocono mountains helping nuns who worked with girls who had been abused. After all the ways I had led girls astray, God gave me these positive opportunities to help. It was a time of purification and grounding in the integrity of God and His word for me. Gradually I began to understand who I was, and how far I had drifted from God's will. It was at this time that my older sister Joy came to visit me with her beautiful family. I can remember taking her out in a boat on the lake with my nephews, whom I love, and sharing with her that I wanted to be a priest. She was gracious, and asked,

"Anthony, with the way you love children, how could you become a priest and not get married?" She reiterated my mother's words of fifteen years earlier, and I realized that I truly wanted to get married and have children. I agreed with her and said, "I don't know how, but I just want to serve the Lord." Marriage and family were very important to me but so was serving God. I knew it was impossible in Catholicism for me to serve full-time and have a family. I shelved the idea of becoming a priest, but the incredible, patient love of Christ kept drawing me closer.

At the end of that summer, Father Charlie approached me with a suggestion. He asked, "Have you ever thought about returning to show business to be a witness for Christ in the nightclubs you came out of just a year and half ago?" "You have to be kidding" was my reply. I was so happy and content serving the Lord where I was, I couldn't comprehend any benefit in returning to show business. What would make me go back to the night life? God's will is always best. After praying, I knew in my spirit what was right, and I returned to show business.

In 1974 I rejoined the band *The Lemon Tree*. During my first engagement back, I was introduced to the woman who was to become my wife, who was in a night club for the first time. Susan was a beautiful and gentle single-parent child. We knew we were in love right from the start, and it didn't take long for me to ask her to marry me. We met in February, and we were married in November of 1974.

From the very start, Susan was a seeker in the things of the Lord even though she did not yet know him as her Savior. She was open to learning. I was continually challenged to help my bride understand the great love of the Father's heart. She had little formal religious training. As newlyweds, we toured the country, traveling from night club to night club. Our trip ended in Las Vegas at the Sahara Hotel. I witnessed about Christ to everyone, and was called "Father Matti" by the members of the group, my stage name being Tony Matti. Waitresses, dancers, blackjack dealers, and rock stars heard the Gospel of Jesus. It was an incredible time, but it was not easy.

In July of 1976 our first baby, James, was born. The little guy traveled all over with us, and my young bride did a tremendous job with him. In 1976, however, while I was appearing in Brockton, Massachusetts, James became sick. His illness was our first real challenge as a married couple. In the midst of a performance I was called from stage because James' coughing seemed dangerous, and Susan didn't know what to do. Not knowing a doctor in the area, and not knowing what to do, I cried out to God, "Lord, I want to be normal. I want a home, a church, and a real job."

I decided to call Father Charlie, since he had started me back in show business. I called the rectory in Mahopac, Charlie's last residence, only to find out he had been transferred to another parish. My heart sank. When I asked "Where to?" I was told he moved to *Brockton, Massachusetts.* I couldn't believe it. I got the number and called him. He helped us get some medicine for the baby's coughing, which turned out to be croup, and in about an hour Charlie, Susan, James, and I were sitting at a table in our hotel restaurant. His counsel to me was clear; he believed that with the birth of our son James, the Lord was saying it was time for us to put down roots.

I felt God's release, and New Year's Eve, 1977, was my last show business performance.

In early 1978, I was introduced to the first church other than a Catholic one. I never had bad feelings toward Catholicism, and still don't. When I returned home I tried to find a Spirit-filled Catholic church like the one in Mahopac, but couldn't. I discovered they were rare. I prayed and felt the Lord speak to me about the church that we were to be a part of. My wife had no church background and really yearned for a basic knowledge of the Lord Jesus and His Word. I believed the church we needed to find was one in which the Word was taught in large dosages. I visited church after church, trying to find *the one.*

God put extraordinary people in my path. He directed me through them to a church called the Full Gospel Tabernacle on Long Island, New York, pastored by David Knapp. Pastor Knapp was a wonderful teacher. The Word of God was the focus of his messages, which confirmed for me that I was in the right place. The church was growing rapidly, and I was asked to work with the youth.

The youth group met in our home. Kids came from everywhere as the church grew. I have always loved children, even teenagers, who "come out of their caves three times a day, eat, grunt, and go back in their caves," as author Charles Shedd has observed in one of his many books. The group was active, and it grew to over a hundred kids. I struggled to minister to all the children. Pastor Knapp noticed the fruit of the Lord in my ministry; the kids applied what I had taught them and grew in the love of the Lord. He invited me into his office one day and said, "I believe there is a call on your life to the ministry. And I think it has been there for a long time." I couldn't believe what I had heard, and I began to cry. I thought about the years of hearing the call of God, but not understanding how God would bring it to pass. Full-time ministry *and* a family — this was too good to be true!

He spoke of my becoming a youth pastor, but I didn't know what that was. He told me to begin to pray for God's direction. When I shared the idea with my wife, she was totally taken back. Susan had married an entertainer, and now he was to be a pastor? "Ministry! I can't be a minister's wife," she exclaimed. One year later the Lord moved on her heart, and she confirmed God's call on my life. I was asked to come on full-time staff with the church as a youth pastor. I had come from the pub to the pew. What an incredible journey! I truly loved working with youth, and as my sensitivity to them grew, I began to notice a group who were beyond my reach, whom I knew needed help. They were single-parent kids. In an attempt to reach them, I became suddenly aware of the depth of their wounds. I knew I didn't have a true understanding of what to do for these kids. I sought out help.

Although I had never been a single parent or a single-parent kid, I knew that the loss of a parent was a major loss in a child's life. I remember as a child not being able to handle the thought of losing my Mom or Dad. The idea hurt too much. I knew these single-parent kids within my pastoral care were hurting, so I sought advice from people about the heartache of the single-parent child. Most of them told me not to worry about the children because they "just bounce back." I knew this was wrong since the single-parent kids in my group trusted me and had shared their pain. I saw children with adult problems. How long would they have to wait to be healed of the incredible loss and pain they felt? Did Jesus have enough compassion for the wounded children to bring healing to them when they were young? Did He want to heal the wounded lambs before they became the lost sheep? I cried out to the Father, "Help me help these children!"

In 1981 God called me to start CHIPS, *Christ's Helpers In Parental Strife.* He gave me the acronym and the logo for it as well. The Lord gave me a vision of the word "CHIPS" with a boldface "I" in the middle. I saw it with the focus on the "I" in the middle. At first, I thought that the Lord was touching me and that I was the "I" in the logo, and I was to touch just the kids of my youth group. I didn't understand the full extent of God's intention regarding the CHIPS ministry. I didn't imagine that the heart of the Father would be shown throughout the land through CHIPS. I knew that God had really spoken to me, but I had no idea of the progressiveness of the vision. I was not looking for anything beyond seeing the single-parent children in my youth group helped and healed. My first attempt to do this was to try to hook up godly men of the fellowship with the boys, so that they would have interaction with positive, Christ-centered role models. Months later, we organized our first CHIPS weekend in which my wife and I, along with several couples, took single-parent children camping for a weekend of encouragement.

After time had passed I began to realize that the "I" in the logo was not me ministering to the youth, but Christ in all believers, the Holy Spirit, who wanted to reach His children. It was as though Christ's body on earth were treating single-parent families as second-class citizens — shunning them. His message, however, was that they were first-class citizens in God's family. They were not "losers." They were winners in Him. And He was touching believers so that we could touch them. It was as though God were telling me, "I am in the middle of your ministry because I am in you." In other words, the Divine Comforter, the one Jesus promised to send as *"another helper"* (John 14:16), is in me to reach and touch the wounded.

In 1985 I left Long Island to become the pastor of family life at the Full Gospel Center in La Grangeville, New York. When I got there, I didn't realize it would be for a short season, just about a year. My time there was prosperous and taught me much, and I believe it was beneficial for the building of the kingdom. As I tried to get a CHIPS ministry going there, I had the privilege of working with some of the finest single-parent families I would ever meet.

While at the La Grangeville church, I booked the team of Mike Cavanaugh and Nancy Honeytree for a single's event at the church. Nancy sang, and Mike preached a dynamic message challenging the single adults. It was following this event that I shared with Mike and Nancy the ministry and vision of CHIPS. Mike was very much interested in CHIPS, and asked if I would consider coming up to Elim Bible Institute in Lima, New York, to join the *Mobilized to Serve* team. *Mobilized to Serve* was one of the leading ministries to single adults in the nation. It seemed CHIPS would fit in with the singles ministry reaching out to the single-parent family.

Within a few months, Susan and I, with our three children and another on the way, moved up to the quaint, rural community of Lima, New York. We joined the staff at Elim Fellowship, a national para-church ministry connected with Elim Bible Institute. It was 1986, and the CHIPS vision was thrust out into the nation. In those days it was tough to be accepted by the church at large because the single-parent issue was rarely addressed, and, furthermore, *who was this Italian guy from the Bronx anyway?* But God revealed His heart, and church by church, conference by conference, people became aware of the Father's heart toward the single-parent household. It felt as though I were spreading the vision liberally every-where, hoping people would receive it. Many did, and we ministered through "Single-Parent Seminars" in a great variety of churches.

The seminars' message of "Wholeness In Christ" was well received, and single parents and chil-dren heard that with Jesus in their house, their home was not broken. We began the CHIPS club for chil-dren. The children were sent a monthly newsletter, a T-shirt, and a membership card. The club's purpose was to let single-parent children know the heavenly Father's love in the midst of their heartache. It was successful as we ministered to many, many children.

It was at this time that we started our CHIPS single-parent camps. At these camps single parents and children came away for a weekend of building new memories. We ministered to the children, as well as to the parents, bringing in the best teachers we could find. The fun and fellowship and faith-build-ing teachings were productive, and many single-parent families were touched in New York, Virginia, Pennsylvania, and Canada.

Ministry opportunities came from everywhere, and I was fully engaged. Single-parent families, whose needs for so long had not been addressed, were now receiving a fresh word from the Lord. The response was very positive. It was especially rewarding to see wounded children healed from the painful experience of divorce. My love for children was blessed, and I became the National Youth Director of Elim Fellowship.

At Elim I was surrounded by men and women of character who helped shape me and knock some of the rough edges off my life. The ministry was draining. I felt like a warship that had gone to sea with bountiful provisions aboard. The ship visited deserted islands, and when it pulled into an island harbor, the natives grabbed at the provisions before it could dock.

In 1992, my family, particularly my first-born son, James, began to show signs of weariness after six years of ministry on the road. He was fifteen, and began acting out in ways that we as a family were not accustomed to seeing. Susan and I felt it was time for me to pull in the sails and to dock. Hopefully, we would settle in a local church. At the same time, Elim was going through a revamping, and the Youth Department vision was being shifted more to the local church. "Where to, Lord?" I prayed, asking the Lord for direction. I got the impression that it would be good for my family to stay close by, so James could finish school at Honeoye Falls-Lima. I believed that pastoring a church nearby that had a Christian school would be the best choice. I wanted to stay close to children, and I loved the thought of seeing little ones every day. During the years I served as National Youth Director, pastors would call for my input about filling youth pastor openings in their churches. One day, I received a call from Pastor Carl Jenks from North Chili Community Church. He asked if I would help him find a replacement for an associate who had just left. The candidate would need some expertise in the area of youth. I heard his request and told him that I would get back to him with a recommendation. When I hung up the phone, I thought, "Who will I send?"

The Lord said, "This is the job for you, Tony." North Chili Community Church had a school and was within traveling distance from Lima. I spoke to Susan, and we thought we would go for it. When I called Carl, much to my surprise, he was excited about the possibility of my joining him on staff at his church.

In May of 1992 we joined the staff of the church in North Chili. During this time of transition and docking, our ship received a broadside hit. In June of 1992 our son James was killed in a car accident, one month before his sixteenth birthday. We were devastated. My love for children in general came from the overflow of love for my own. The loss of James hit me at the core of my being as a man, father, and minister. I thought I would never recover from the loss. I thank God that He had put us in a safe harbor, a local church of tremendously loving people. It took a long time to recover, but five years after James's death, I was able to say, "The Lord is faithful." My family and I have come through the pain successfully, recognizing that faith in Jesus Christ works. The intensity of my grief drove me to a deeper understanding of loss. Before losing James, I thought I understood loss and heartache, but not the way I do now. I am now able to say to single parents, "God will bring you through your pain as well. He will teach you in it, and you will grow through it."

During our time of grief, I ministered very little with CHIPS. I was in tremendous pain. A church in Australia read an article I had written in *Charisma* magazine and asked if I would bring the vision and ministry of CHIPS to the land down under. I did, and to this day, I've returned each year. I've watched the ministry grow in the southern hemisphere.

CHIPS today has its headquarters at New Covenant Community Church in Audubon, New Jersey, where I have been the pastor since 1998. CHIPS has ministered to multitudes of single-parent households in countries around the world. Our annual single-parent camps have been sold out each year. Our monthly CHIPS meetings have drawn over 350 single-parent families per year.

Chapter Three

WHAT THE BIBLE HAS TO SAY ABOUT SINGLE-PARENT FAMILIES

If you were to study a concordance to find out what the Bible has to say about single parenting, you might come away frustrated in your effort. The concordance lists no passages in the Bible dealing with single parenting directly, but the good news is that God's truths apply to all of life. They apply to you regardless of your marital status. God does speak in His Holy Word to the single parent, and his message is powerful.

As God increased my desire to reach out to single-parent families, I became impatient as I waited for Him to show me His perspective on the matter. I discovered verses here and there about widows and orphans, about God's concern for the fatherless, the lonely and the desolate, but I was hungry for a coherent word from God upon which He would establish a ministry.

As usual, God did not disappoint me, but the passages He brought to my attention were a bit of a surprise because they did not appear to be talking about single-parent families, at first. They demonstrate something that all believers must understand. While many Biblical passages address a matter directly—for example, the "thou shalt not's" of the Ten Commandments—more often, the Bible presents principles in a metaphoric way, as stories that we can apply to our personal situation with the help of the Holy Spirit even though the problems we are facing do not exactly match the circumstance in scripture. Jesus taught in parables, stories that illustrated a principle. As he spoke, the Holy Spirit, working in the hearts and minds of the hearers, enlightened each person as to the truth that the Lord wanted him or her to understand. In the same way, other stories that God has recorded in His Word reveal principles that apply to all of our lives. In I Corinthians 10:6, Paul tells us that these stories were recorded in the scriptures as "examples" (types or models) for us: *"Now these things happened as examples for us, that we should not crave evil things, as [the Israelites when they were in the desert] also craved."*

In other words, when you read a story in the Bible, it may seem to be just a historical account of some event. But God intends that it be more than that. These events are meant as illustrations of truth, and we need the Holy Spirit, working through our minds and circumstances to show their relevance to us. When Jesus said, *"Let them that have ears hear"* (Matthew 11:15), He was saying, "Let them whose understanding is being guided by the Holy Spirit discern the spiritual truth in what I am saying."

I searched the Scriptures over several months trying to understand God's perspective on single-parent families. I kept finding myself drawn to the Book of Lamentations, but for the longest time I couldn't understand why. The passages I was drawn to had to do with the city of Jerusalem, not with single parents. What was God saying to me?

Finally when God got through to me, I was overwhelmed. He not only got through to my mind, but He touched my heart with His attitude toward the desperate state of the tormented families of Jerusalem. After you read this chapter, take some time to read the Book of Lamentations at your first opportunity. As you read, note how what is written speaks to your situation as a single-parent family— particularly the underlying emotions of what is being described. Look at the first verse of chapter 1:

> *How lonely sits the city*
> *That was full of people!*
> *She has become like a widow*
> *Who was once great among the nations!*
> *She who was a princess among the provinces*
> *Has become a forced laborer!*

This verse can be paraphrased to reflect the circumstances of the single parent:

How lonely sits the single parent
Whose home was once filled with company
She has become weighted down with grief
She who was accepted and respected in her
> *community*
and loved among her family
Now has no time, no friends,
And is forced to work for pennies.

Let us take a closer look at each part of Lamentations 1:1.

How lonely sits the city...

What a statement from the writer of Lamentations, whom most scholars consider to be Jeremiah, viewing the ruined city of Jerusalem! The words reflect the heart of our Father. Jerusalem was considered the "crown jewel" of the nation, a city of special interest to God, and yet it stood in ruins. The very city where the Holy One resided in the Temple now seemed to be worth nothing, destroyed by the Babylonian army.

As I consider the lament for the ruined city, my heart joins with the Father's cry for the people — parents losing their homes, children losing their parents. Suffering and heartache are everywhere; dreams are crushed by the enemy's victory. *"Oh, how lonely sits the city."* It is no wonder that Jeremiah is called the weeping prophet. How appropriate that the weeping prophet would address issues that are relevant to single-parent families — I don't think that it is mere coincidence that the impact of our CHIPS seminars is sometimes measured by how many boxes of tissues we use! As I speak tears are everywhere.

As I let my imagination take in the scene that these verses describe, I am struck by the similarity between the mood of these passages and the feelings of single parents, especially those who have recently experienced divorce. The pain, the loneliness, the loss of vitality, the absence of joy and laughter, the low self-esteem, and negative self-image, all parallel the image of the desolated city. It is as though they have been reduced from the elevated position of a princess at the time of the wedding to the lowly estate of a social outcast.

When theologians describe Jerusalem's destruction in 586 BC by the Babylonians, they typically portray the city as a widow in mourning. When Jerusalem again suffered destruction at the hands of the Romans in 70 AD, the Roman General Titus erected an arch of triumph to commemorate his conquest. On the arch, Jerusalem was depicted as a weeping, disheveled woman, seated upon the ground mourning. Where once Jehovah had set His name, now stood a ruined city, looked upon with broken heart and tearful eye. A city once filled with joy, hope, and vision, was now devastated by warfare—its temple destroyed.

As the Holy Spirit has sensitized my heart toward the things of God's Kingdom and His people, I have seen that this type warfare still continues. The same tactics that were used by the Babylonians in the physical warfare against Jerusalem are being used by Satan in the spiritual warfare against families today.

The Babylonians' ultimate goal was not the city walls. The walls were just the initial target. The fall of the temple was the ultimate goal (see Illustration #1). When the temple fell, the Babylonians had effec

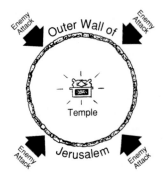

Illustration #1

RUIN THE CITY/DESTROY THE TEMPLE

The enemy's attack breaks through the protective wall ultimately, to destroy the Temple.

Illustration #2

The institution of marriage is a protective place for the souls of the family.

tively separated the Jews from their God. And so it has been with our enemy, Satan, since the creation of mankind. His purpose has always been to turn people away from God. With Eve and Adam in the garden, the serpent was not out to change people's perspective on fruit! He was trying to destroy their fellowship with God.

So the situation is today. The statistics clearly demonstrate that marriage is under attack. The enemy is working to break down the protective "wall" of marriage and the family unit—the unity of husband and wife and children. But his ultimate target is each individual soul (see Illustration #2). His objective is to turn the individuals away from fellowship with God: to encourage the father to run away from his responsibilities, to submerge the mother in depression, and to rob the children of security and perhaps propel them into rebellion. It's not necessarily the initial breakup of the family itself that brings the most pain to the individuals. Instead, the individuals get ensnared by the poor or even sinful life-impacting choices that they make in the aftermath of the breakup. These choices push them into the concentration camps of despair and aimless existence. When this is compounded by a turning away by the body of Christ from these wounded ones, the enemy has clear sailing to triumph over the hopeless individuals (see Illustration #3).

Illustration #3

RUIN THE CITY/DESTROY THE TEMPLE

A marriage is much like the outer walls of Jerusalem. Should the enemy break up the marriage, the Temple or souls are able to be captured by the enemy.

People suffering can be described as living in caves of fear, continuing in the loss of the joy of living and of their trust in God. This concept is typified in the life of an obese single-parent who came to talk with me. She related how she had been utterly alone, having no relationship with anyone. She was obviously hurting, but she went on to say that she had just realized that she preferred it that way. She talked about her failed attempts to lose weight, and after attending a seminar she now knew why she was unable to diet successfully. She said her obesity helped her "to alienate others and keep them at arm's length." She had successfully shut herself inside a fortress of obesity because of her fear of relationships. In the process, she had removed herself further and further from the lifeline of the fellowship she so desperately needed. The enemy working through her fear had put her in a cave-like existence.

Such loneliness is the antithesis of fellowship, and it's where the enemy wants the single-parent family to reside. In the first book of Kings we see that even the mighty prophet of God, Elijah, experienced loneliness caused by fear. After his spectacular and miraculous defeat of the prophets of Baal, Jezebel threatened him, and he was suddenly gripped with fear. Fear drove him, and he ran for his life into the wilderness. Now, in total isolation from people, his fear became so overpowering that he was blinded by it. Even the appearance of the angel of God in the wilderness bringing him food was not enough to capture his attention and draw him into fellowship with his Lord. Likewise, the Lord shows His concern for us in our wildernesses, but we are often so blinded by fear that we too miss His hand of provision.

Eventually, Elijah ended up, literally, in a cave, the ultimate residence of isolation and loneliness. So it is with many single parents. In reaction to their fear, they withdraw into a cave-like existence, imagining that this is better than risking the potential hurts that are an inevitable part of all human interaction. Fortunately, God's Word can reach inside a cave. God spoke to Elijah, and he overcame his fears and returned to the work of the Lord.

Just as God spoke to the woman who had locked herself in a cave of obesity, and set her free to risk experiencing fellowship again, you as a single parent do not have to stay in your cave. That's not where God wants you; that's where Satan wants you. Getting back into the flow of life is necessary, and hopefully this book will help you do it!

She has become like a widow...

In the first verse of Lamentations 1, Jeremiah says the city *"has become like a widow."* What image is brought to your mind? Isn't it an image of a person drained of her vitality, as though she had lost her reason for living? It reminds me of David's words from Psalm 32:3-4, *"...My body wasted away...My vitality was drained away as with the fever heat of summer."*

Many single parents exist in a state of drained vitality: physically, emotionally and spiritually. Like grieving widows, their lives are characterized by depression. In many ways there is little about their existence that speaks of real life. What then do we make of Jesus' declaration that He came to bring not only life, but abundant life? Can vitality be restored to the life of the single parent? The answer is a definite "Yes," but the means of achieving it may come as something of a surprise. He restores our vitality by forgiving our sins as we confess them to Him. Why was David wasting away and feeling the loss of His vitality? The psalm starts out with David declaring that this heaviness descended upon him *"when I kept silent about my sin..."* (Psalm 32:3). And how was he restored? *"I said, 'I will confess my transgressions to the Lord,' and You forgave the guilt of my sin"* (verse 5). At that point David regained his vitality and was invigorated by the awareness of God's mercy and love for him, which restored to him a position of righteousness before God. He says in Psalm 32:11, "Be glad in the Lord and rejoice, you righteous ones, and shout for joy, all you who are upright in heart." Wouldn't you like to move from your heaviness and sorrow into a condition where you feel fully alive and feel like rejoicing and shouting for joy? Then follow David's example.

"But, wait a minute," the single parent may be saying. "It isn't sin that's causing my depression — at least, not my sin! I'm depressed because of what was done to me, and what was taken from me." I won't argue that you have not been victimized. I wish you never had gone through the heartache that has come to you. I wish you did not need to go through the normal process of grieving, of which depression is a normal part. Too many Christians have criticized people who have been traumatized because they weren't cheery and smiling. However, if after the normal process is completed, you continue to be depressed, then you must look for an additional cause. Let's take a closer look at the statement above about sin not being the cause of the single parent's depression. Isn't it an admission that such depression is derived from bitterness? On-going depression is not a result of what happens to us, but of our reaction to what happens to us. Can we go through heartache and loss in life and still emerge with joy? Yes, we can, but it does not come immediately. Joy will come eventually if you deal with the bitterness successfully through forgiving. The flip side to receiving life by asking God to forgive our sins is to forgive those who have sinned against us. You must learn to forgive the ones who have hurt you.

Consider the example of Jesus. Jesus — the only completely innocent man ever to have lived — was betrayed, arrested under false pretenses, abused physically and verbally, and humiliated by hanging before the public naked but for a loin cloth. He was condemned without guilt to one of the cruelest forms of execution ever devised, and he was killed for sins He never committed. What does the Bible say about His attitude as an example to us? *"For consider Him who endured such hostility by sinners against Himself, so that you may not grow weary and lose heart"* (Hebrews 12:3). What was Jesus' attitude? The Bible tells us that Jesus was one *"...who, for the joy set before Him endured the cross, despising the shame, and has sat down at the right hand of the throne of God"* (Hebrews 12:2). The "joy" that Jesus was looking forward to was to come as a result of His being put to death to purchase forgiveness and redemption for the very ones who were unjustly killing Him! What is the sin that produces depression when we have been wronged? Unforgiveness. Where does joy and renewed vitality come from? Forgiveness.

How do I get to the point of being able to forgive? It's by acknowledging my own sin, accepting Jesus' forgiveness of me and then letting that grace

and mercy extend to those who have wronged me.
You and I are sinners. We are not innocent. Many
single parents have described themselves to me as
completely innocent as they have talked of the
breakup of a marriage. I understand what they
mean, and my compassion for their hurt makes me
want to believe them. But I know that their version
of the facts is likely something of a distortion of reali-
ty. There may be differing degrees of guilt — one
party is often more guilty than the other — but there
is rarely total innocence on one person's part
because we are all sinners.

There is a tendency to look at other people
and point our fingers. "Oh, pastor, if you knew him,
you'd understand. His mother ruined him. His job,
those friends, that golf." Remember, when you point
your finger, three of your fingers are pointing back at
you. We must accept the responsibility for our own
shortcomings. When we do, then God can forgive us.

Forgiveness does not consist of merely saying,
"I forgive you." Rather, it involves a profound change
of heart toward the offender and a willingness to
intercede on his or her behalf. I have had single parents and, sadly, even some of their children tell me,
"I've forgiven him, and as far as I'm concerned, he's
dead!" Is this forgiveness the kind that Jesus demonstrated? Did Jesus say, "O.K., I've died for them.
That's enough. Now, Father, deal with them." In frustration Jesus did not say, "I'm not about to spend any
time in the tomb to get eternal life for this pack of
murderers! That's it. I've had it with these sinners."
Not at all! In fact, He visited hell, totally defeating
the enemy and took the keys of life and death and
restored to us our victory. Freedom and eternal life

is available to those who truly confess Jesus, if they repent and call upon His name as Savior. If you cry out in your sin, He is faithful to forgive your sin and cleanse you from all unrighteousness, as I John 1:9 tells us. What a heart! Let us consider what Jesus has been doing ever since His resurrection and ascension. He *"always lives to make intercession for [sinners]"* (Hebrews 7:25). He is praying that none will be lost. How about you? Have you asked God to forgive you? What are your actions toward those people whom you claim to have forgiven? Is your heart open to blessing others as the Lord leads? Are you praying for God's grace and blessing for them, even if they have hurt you?

Genuine, mature forgiveness has three steps— forgiving, having a change in heart, and intercessory praying— as seen in the redeeming work of Jesus Christ. He went to the cross to win forgiveness for sinners. He rose from the dead to win blessings for sinners. And He sits at God's right hand to intercede (pray) for sinners. The Bible teaches us that we must be crucified with Christ, resurrected with Christ, and seated with Christ. We show that these things have occurred in our lives when, like Christ, we are able to forgive, bless, and pray for those who have hurt us. Who is better able to pray for your ex-spouse's needs than you? Who knows his or her faults and short-comings better than you? What an intercessor you can be! You can achieve a heavenly perspective, seated in a heavenly place with Jesus, as you intercede for your ex-spouse.

One experience of great benefit in the life of single-parent children is for them to witness the willingness of their parents to grow in forgiveness for one another. As forgiveness flows, parents can look at the children who still love their mother and father and ask themselves, "What do the children need in order to grow into emotionally healthy and happy human beings?" Many a single-parent child is placed in the middle of tremendous warfare by parents. One or both parents cannot accept the decision to divorce, so the battle continues.

The enemy thinks, "All I have to do is hit the family. If I hit the family, I can take the souls." But you are going to frustrate him by stepping on his neck and saying, "You may have hit my family, but you're not going to take my soul or my children's souls!" Then deliver another hit to the enemy by saying, "I'm even going to start interceding for the soul of my ex-spouse! I have discovered that there is something even more important than this earthly relationship. I have an eternal one."

ANGER

At the place of impact in the "wall" of our existence, where the heartache hits us, people can make a choice to act or react. People caught in their pain receive input at the place of impact both from the Lord and the devil. At such a time, anger is a normal emotion. When people are hurt and are not free from the pain of the wound, they remain in their loss, and anger is the product of this unresolved grief. We are all prone to anger and susceptible to its pull. How far do we let it go? How long should we remain angry? How can we rid ourselves of this powerful emotion and its negative effects? The answer depends on whose voice we listen to, God's or Satan's. God's Word says, "*Be angry and yet do not sin, do not let the sun go down on your anger, and do not give the devil an opportunity"* (Ephesians 4:26-27). The Lord knows we will get angry. His instruction that anger must be righteous applies 24 hours a day. We should not stew in our anger, day after day until we boil over splattering the boiling water outside ourselves and scalding those around us. Hard choices in life are always going to challenge us to grow and make the right choice.

HOW TO RESPOND TO THE IMPACT

Times of impact occur many times in a lifetime. We are challenged to make a choice on how to respond to difficult and sometimes painful circumstances. The place of impact is a place of major decision that will influence your future — a place of loss of life, relationship, or job. We must chose God's way when we are at the place of impact. The impact place offers two directions we can follow: life or death, the blessing or a curse. When God gave the ten commandments to the Israelites, he said,

> *"I call heaven and earth to witness against you today, that I have set before you life and death, the blessing and the curse. So choose life in order that you may live, you and your descendants, by loving the Lord you God, by obeying His voice, and by holding fast to Him"* (Deuteronomy 30:19-20).

At this crossroads, this place of decision-making, people can fall into foolishness or into wisdom. Fools react to whatever they feel, thinking that it is not against God's will for them to be angry. It's natural, and it feels good, so why not give full vent to the anger? They believe they have license to say whatever pops into their mind, to do whatever, throw whatever! They profess to be wise in their reactions, but really they are fools.

They are fools because they have followed the way of the curse and death, and although it feels good at the moment, it will lead to hell on earth. They play the fool believing the lie as truth. They become deceived. The person who falls for an April fool joke, whether intended as a light-hearted teasing or as a more serious deception, is taken into the lie, hook, line, and sinker. He really believes it is true until someone says, "April Fool!" If you have ever been the brunt of the joke, you can remember the feeling of the blood running from your face as you realize you've believed a lie. The enemy wants us to play the fool, and he tempts us with his lies to see if we will take the bait. The place of impact is an opportune place for this to occur because we are sus-ceptible. We then become susceptible to additional problems because anger is a "gateway" emotion — it opens the door to bitterness and hatred, violence, and vengeance. Jesus' place of impact was the cross of Calvary. When we look to Him, for example, we see how He handled the pressure. He handled it God's way.

At the crossroads, or crisis points, or places of impact in our lives, we must learn to do things God's way. We give up our will and submit ourselves to act out His will. If, as it says in Galatians 2:20, *"we have been crucified with Christ, and we no longer live but Christ lives in us,"* then at the crossroads we need to respond as Jesus would, and then others will see Jesus in us. Jesus on the cross did not respond in anger. He did not retaliate. We need to respond according to

Jesus' words in Matthew 5:43: *"You have heard it said you shall love your neighbor and hate your enemies but I say love your enemies and pray for those who persecute you."* To follow this verse is to chose the blessing rather than the curse at the point of impact— not "I'll bless him with a brick," but true blessing to those who perse-cute you, done in the way that the Lord leads you. I'm not saying you should run out and buy flowers to give your enemy without consulting the Lord, but I am saying that you should stay open to the Lord's direction. Keep open to godly counsel and guidance. The fool for Christ is the winner in any situation. As we line up with His word, our victory will come.

When you are harassed by painful memories, pray through them by lifting up the one who has wrongfully used you. The enemy will soon cease harassing you, knowing that every time he reminds you of the past, you intercede for the offender. This will curb your anger and seat you in a heavenly place with Christ Jesus. You will prove what God's Word says in Proverbs16:32, *"He who is slow to anger is better than the mighty."*

Anger ultimately looks for an opportunity to take revenge. You need to be vigilant. Unresolved anger that spills out to hurt or retaliate will look for the opportune time to explode. It is different from unresolved grief in that unresolved grief still is in the healing process and is not looking to strike out but rather to understand. For example, if you're a unwed single mother who never sees the child's father any more, the memory of the abandonment can still carry great pain. The loss of your future promise and your plans can continually be a thorn in your heart. Remember who holds your future. Consider that the one who says *"Vengeance is mine. I will repay"* (Hebrews 10:30) will not only deal with the offender but return to the offended what has been lost. It may come in a different way than what you have envisioned, but trust that He will repay. He holds the keys to the future for you and your children. Vengeance is not the answer. One single parent wrote me about her thoughts on vengeance:

> There is a tendency in break-ups in which one of us hangs on to our faith and the other abandons it to 'do his own thing,' for the 'righteous' one to feel justified in keeping the kids safe in a nice protected Christian environment. 'It's not good for the kids to be exposed to their daddy (mommy) and the un-Christian lifestyle,' we want to tell ourselves. 'We must protect them from harm,' we think. On the surface this sounds good. However, we must ask some heavy and deep-seated questions about motive and, before God, answer honestly. Christians and non-Christians both counseled me not to allow my ex to see the kids so much. 'He doesn't deserve to have them,' they'd say. Perhaps they were right in a strictly legal sense. However, forgiveness isn't concerned with what's strictly right, wrong, or deserved. And love (for God and the children) overlooks the hurt and desire to see the rat get what he deserves! Forgiveness means the forgiver takes the lumps that the offender deserves. As a Christian, then, we don't say, 'You left, you reneged on your vows, and you'll pay by not seeing the kids.' Rather, we say, 'You left, you reneged on your vows, and, even though I've been wronged, and you are the one who should

pay a price, I will exact no price.' In that, we dump it into God's lap where it rightly belongs. Then we are free to look at the little children who still love their daddy, who want to be with him to be loved, cuddled, and bounced, and say, 'What do they really need and want in order to grow into emotionally whole and fulfilled human beings?' Let God take care of the 'tally' of the ex. You who are sinned against have the responsibility not for punishing but for forgiving, walking wherever and however God leads, and loving the one who hurt you so deeply. In this there is fullness of joy.

What about your household? Is there fullness of joy there? Is your household like Jerusalem, *"that was full of people"* (Lamentations 1:1), a place of gathering and celebration, where traditional holidays were observed with great festivity before the enemy attacked, but which then became a place of mourning and desolation? In the same way, a single-parent household can become a sullen environment. The heartbreak of divorce or a spouse's death registers very high on the scale of emotional trauma. Joy can disappear quickly and laughter be relegated to things of the past. Single parents must carefully guard their joy.

That many single parents face a listless, joyless existence is truly unfortunate for through Jesus Christ life *can* be turned around. How quickly? As quickly as you want. And for the sake of your children, it is important for you to ask God to help you let him turn your life around. In the parent and child relationship, children imitate the behavior modeled by their parents. They can "die" emotionally because of the choices that the parents make with regard to yielding to the Lord's help. In the story of Elijah in I Kings 17, a single parent at Zarephath was about to cook her last meal and as far as she knew die. It was not only she who would die, but her son, too. For his sake, she needed God's intervention. In Genesis 21, when Hagar ran out of the provisions that Abraham had given her, it was not only she that was going to die; it was her son Ishmael as well. When a single parent decides to live his or her life in the doldrums of sadness and to pitch a tent in the valley of the shadow of death, the quality of life for the children suffers. The ill effects can then be passed on to their children.

Perhaps your home used to be a place where friends and family gathered for fellowship and celebration, filled with joy and laughter, *before* the enemy attacked. You must fight by denying yourself and by seeing things with God's perspective and responding obediently to His word and His way if you ever hope to see family health restored. Then you will get joy and laughter back in your home.

Many single parents I have met appear to limp along in life with a "poor me" attitude. "I used to be happy. I used to laugh," they say, suggesting that joy is a bygone, permanently lost thing. Meanwhile, their children are growing up in a desert experience that they are learning to accept as "normal" life. Even Christian parents who have gone through the impact of such tragedy can lose their perspective and forget that joy should be the norm in the Christian life. While most people take laughter for granted, badly hurt people sometimes have to learn to laugh all over again. That's why in our CHIPS weekends, where we focus on wholeness in God, we include many things to help single parents and their children rediscover fun together. After one such weekend a single mother came to me and said, "Saturday afternoon, during the Double Dare, I laughed so much I was crying. You know, I haven't laughed in 15 years with my children!" She and her family were well on their way to wholeness again.

Many single parents are so bent on being "good parents" and having "good children" that they totally miss the joy of parenting and under the pressure of parenting are robbing their children of the joy of childhood. They seem always to be correcting and disciplining their children. Their kids are under a constant verbal barrage of "Don't do this! Do this! Don't do that!" They seem incapable of enjoying their children. If you think you are uptight, then chances are you're trying too hard to be both Mom and Dad. Don't do it. You can't. Just be the best mom you can be, or the best dad you can be, and let God fill the void and bridge the gap. By trying so hard to be what you never can be, you'll most likely fail at what you can be. Your kids need you to be healthy in the role that is properly yours. Trying to fill both roles will only fracture you, and it is not expected of you.

One single mother came to me for counseling, saying, "I can't get my sons to communicate with me." I could see that this woman was really stiff. In fact, she was so uptight she almost made my lips pucker like when I bite a lemon! I said, "If you're willing to try a different approach, I believe you will get your boys talking to you again. Do you own a pair of sneakers?" She said she did. "Then put them on,

exchange a ten-dollar bill for a roll of quarters, take
your sons to a mall and go to the video arcade."
"Oh, Tony! Ten dollars is so precious on our little
budget!" she protested. "Listen to me," I persisted.
"You asked me for advice. Now try my suggestion."
Six months passed before I saw her again at a singles
conference. "Tony, you won't believe what happened," she bubbled. "I did what you said, and as
we left the arcade and were walking in the mall, a
conversation started and it hasn't ended yet. We're
still talking!"

Single parent, lighten up! Get a roll of quarters, get down to your child's level, relate to them,
and enjoy them and life. Work at laughter. If you
can't think of anything better, get some funny
movies. Enjoy the Three Stooges. Watch as a family,
and release your laughter.

...Who was once great among the nations...

Like Jerusalem, *"Who was once great among the
nations...who was a princess among the provinces"* and now
"has become a forced laborer" (Lamentations 1:1), many
single parents suffer from a loss of self-esteem, and
they struggle with a low self-image. If the insensitivity
of people whom you trusted and loved has tainted or
smashed your self-image, take heart. God is the Master Image-Builder. In fact, He is the only One who
truly knows in whose image you were made. He
formed you in the womb with a purpose and a destiny.

As we pass through life, there are many influences that work to deform and defeat us: trials, tribu-
lation, harsh words said, deeds done, and things we
ourselves have said and done. We must guard
against letting wrong input shape us into that which

does not bring glory to God. Jesus brings glory to God, and as God's child, you are *"predestined to become conformed to the image of His Son"* (Romans 8: 29). Letting the image of Christ take shape in us glorifies God and overcomes the other influences that work to destroy our self-esteem. Maybe you have been attacked with words like, "You never knew how to love!" or "You're a loser!" or "You never satisfied me!" or "I hate you!" If you let them, such words can bind and capture you emotionally, twisting your self-concept and robbing you of your heavenly calling.

Your defense against such attacks is to keep before you the view that God has of you. He knows your imperfections, but He does not despise you. He loves you so much that He was willing to give His own life for you. He who formed you, came to earth and lived for you, died for you, and rose for you, is still on your side. He is for you. As the writer of Romans said, *"If God is for us, who is against us?"* (Romans 8:31). If the One who is the center of the universe considers you worthy of His love, does it really matter, ultimately, if a mere person writes you off as unlovable? Is his or her opinion superior to God's?

One result of harboring a negative self-image is to push others away. Jesus says to you, "I love you. Don't push me away. I long to embrace you. *You are embraceable.* My vision is larger than yours, and my power is available to turn even that which is evil to good. You are my masterpiece."

Don't settle for being like a "forced laborer," one who is "under the circumstances." Rise above the circumstances by doing everything as unto the Lord. *"Whatever you do, do all to the glory of God"*

(I Corinthians 10:31). Don't let disappointment drive you into a cave of despair. Determine that, in God, you will grow, not wither; decide to expand, not shrivel.

You need to take action to help get yourself out of the doldrums. Look for ways to expand your education. Look for wholesome ways to bring excitement to your life and the life of your children. Expand your horizons of friendship by aggressively seeking opportunities for interaction with people. Don't wait to be reached out to. Reach out to others. Extend an invitation to someone. Seek to become a positive influence in the life of others. Release joy by becoming a worshipper. In the presence of the Holy Spirit there is fullness of joy. Our Lord inhabits the praises of His people. If you will latch on firmly to the truth as God perceives it, you will find life to be an exciting adventure with your Friend always at your side declaring, *"I will never desert you, nor will I ever forsake you"* (Joshua 1:5 NIV).

Chapter Four

CHILDREN UNDER SIEGE

As we have seen, the enemy's strategy of attacking the family is illustrated in Lamentations. I see Lamentations as the heart-cry of children caught in the midst of war, and, as Jeremiah's heart broke for these children, so does mine:

> *"For these things I weep;*
> *My eyes run down with water;*
> *Because far from me is a comforter*
> *One who restores my soul;*
> *My children are desolate*
> *Because the enemy has prevailed"*
> (Lamentations 1:16)

My paraphrase for single parents:

> *In this I cry tears of great pain*
> *For no one is near to comfort me.*
> *No one who cares*

and would take the time to help me
My children suffer
because bad and evil have triumphed.

This verse says that *"the enemy has prevailed."* Why does the enemy prevail? In this verse the writer says that the enemy prevails with the children because a comforter who restores their soul is not there for them. Who is this comforter who restores souls? The Word of God says that the Holy Spirit is called the Comforter. Where does the awesome spiritual power of the Holy Spirit abide? The question is answered in John 14:16 where the writer states that the Spirit will abide with you.

Another reason that the enemy prevails is that the church avoids his victims because we would have to go inside the war zone to rescue them. Nevertheless, we should use the authority and boldness that are available to us in the Lord to fearlessly pursue them into the war zone in love and set the captive little ones free, free to grow in God and be all He has destined them to be.

We hear the agony of defeat in the first chapter of Lamentations as we hear children wail to God. The complaint continues in Lamentations 5:1-7:

"Remember, O Lord, what has befallen us;
Look, and see our reproach!
Our inheritance has been turned over to strangers,
Our houses to aliens.
We have become orphans without a father,
Our mothers are like widows.
We have to pay for our drinking water,

Our wood comes to us at a price.
Our pursuers are at our necks;
We are worn out, there is no rest for us.
We have submitted to Egypt and Assyria to get
    enough bread.
Our fathers sinned, and are no more;
It is we who have borne their iniquities."

My paraphrase for single parents:

Hey, God, look over here.
Can't you see that our hearts are broken?
That which was saved for us has been turned over
    to others.
The place in which we grew up has been sold
    to strangers.
We are the fatherless.
Our mothers are in so much pain.
Nothing comes to us cheaply;
Necessities are so expensive.
It seems like we are under attack.
We are so weary;
We have sought help from anyone who will offer,
And our only help has come from the dark side.
Our fathers screwed up,
And we are paying the price of their sin.
It's unfair.

Many theologians see the book of Lamentations only as the desperation of a widow, or more generally, a weeping woman. As the Lord revealed this heart-cry of the children in Lamentations to me, I saw parents and children, weeping and hungry, homeless and hurting. I began to see not only an adult left without a mate, but also children left without one or both parents. I saw a single-parent family. I saw children suffering as a result of parental strife. The Book of Lamentations began to open up to me. I understood the heart of the Father toward the children who are exposed to the enemy's attack. Let's take a closer look at each part of Lamentations 5:1-7:

Remember, O Lord, what has befallen us; Look, and see our reproach!

The cry of the children in Lamentations 5:1 is so typical of single-parent children today. Many feel as though the Lord has forgotten them. It's as if they have to remind God, "Lord I'm here! Remember me? God, can you see what has come upon us? It's a disgrace. Pay attention to what has come against us." Many children at the time of the enemy's attack believe that the Lord has forsaken them. It's as though their prayers and tears in the night have gone unanswered. They've become alienated from the Christian world and the healing influence of the Holy Spirit.

The problem is compounded as parents justify their actions and further damage the child's faith. For example, a 10-year old at a CHIPS weekend shared, "My father said God told him to divorce my mother." With tears streaming down his cheeks, he asked, "Why would God do such a thing? I hated God for that, but now I know God didn't tell my parents to split up." Do you hear the intensity and cruelty of the enemy's attack on the character of God the Father? Do you hear the lie?

The enemy goes after the lambs to destroy, reject, and alienate them from their heavenly Father. An earthly father's love is so wonderful when it's right, and it points the child's heart toward the Lord. However, when parental strife comes, the father image of God is distorted because of the sinful behavior of the natural father. Promises are not kept, responsibilities are not lived up to, and the child's love and trust seems to be squashed by harsh emotions. The results are devastating because children see God the Father as one who resembles their natural father. Ideally the family unit is designed to bring a sense of well being to the lives of those in it. The harmony of husband and wife should exemplify the love Christ has for His church. Children who do not experience harmony and are caught in the midst of parental strife may think, "If that's what God's love is all about, I don't want it. If God were really God, He would stop this ungodly home life."

One young adolescent in Canada came to the altar with her pastor at a seminar. The pastor asked me to look at her hands. Much to my surprise, the skin from her hands had been peeled away, leaving a hot pink glow to her hands. She had been ripping at herself. I asked her, "Child what are you doing to yourself? What is the pain so deep in your heart?" She blurted out through tears, "I hate my father!" I held her to my heart and stayed there for fifteen minutes while she wept and wept. As her tears subsided, I told her that as much as she felt hatred, her heart truly wanted a father to love, but he had terribly disappointed her. I explained to her that the heart was not made to hate but to love. I shared how the pain of her wounded heart was very real and that she needed to turn to the Maker of the heart to help her understand what she felt, then allow Him to cleanse and repair the heart He so wonderfully designed to love. I shared with her how each of us have had imperfect parents, how being a parent has a lot to do with how you were parented, and that many parents don't know the right thing to do. This truth should drive us to the perfect parent — our Heavenly Father. She bowed her head and released forgiveness for the hatred she held in her heart toward her dad. Months later, I saw the pastor. When I asked, "How is the young lady?" I was told, "She has been healed from the day you prayed, Tony. She has forgiven her dad and miraculously she has stopped ripping at herself."

Our inheritance has been turned over to strangers... We have to pay for our drinking water, Our wood comes to us at a price. Our pursuers are at our necks...

"Things here are not too secure, Lord. I have nothing to fall back on. Familiar things are gone." Finances and the accumulation of some earthly treasures are important to our sense of security. The lack of finances puts many a family on the welfare rolls, living with less than they had been accustomed to before the divorce. When the possibility of financial insecurity and loss affect us, it can cause tremendous emotional insecurity. If left to fester, this insecurity can result in unhealthy character development and emotional immaturity. Many youth feel that they are doomed to nothingness when all the riches of the family are divided between feuding parents and then their portion is sold just to eke out an existence. This upheaval compounds the normal developmental changes which make youth unsure of themselves especially during adolescence. A no-hope attitude can arise which projects nothing but doom and gloom. This attitude affects school work and social behavior drastically. Studies have shown that the single-parent child is five times more susceptible to being suspended or expelled from school, and two times more susceptible to repeating grades during or after a divorce than other children are.

The possibility of losing your inheritance really takes shape in the life of the single-parent child when one parent remarries and step-children are involved. The bitterness which enters the heart of the child has its roots in jealousy and insecurity. The idea of others having the relationships, possessions, and parents that once belonged solely to him makes a child feel resentment. Visiting the home of the non-custodial parent can put a child in a place of greater frustration than we can imagine. For the most part, children don't experience the joy of a step-family; a step-family only brings more stress. To illustrate this point, here is the testimony of a thirteen-year old girl that was published in one of the CHIPS newsletters:

> **"My parents divorced almost four years ago, but it seems like it's been all my 13 years. At first I felt scared and thought my life would never be good again. I cried a lot, thinking of how my life would be. But God was with us every minute, being our Dad because ours had left. We trusted in Him, and He provided all we needed. He cared for us and brought us**

through. I can't even imagine what my life would be like without the love of God that pulled us through. My father remarried about seven months ago. His new wife has a seven year-old boy. His parents divorced when he was four or five. He is troubled about this and is not always easy to get along with. He is happy with his mother's remarriage and wants to call my father 'Dad.' It hurts me and I feel like he might take my dad away. He wants to change his last name to mine. This upsets me. I don't know how I should feel. But I know the Lord is going to help me through this situation. What everything wraps up to is 'Trust in the Lord with all your heart, and He will help you. He'll never leave you nor forsake you.' I thank Him and give Him the praise for all He has done for my family and me."

As you can likely sense from this child's words, she was concerned with the loss of her inheritance of dreams. Not only was she concerned about her inheritance, but her name had been turned over to strangers.

Many parents in a new marriage push their children too quickly into relationships with the new spouse or step-children. They expect their children to have the same feelings they have toward the new spouse and his or her children but are disconcerted when they don't. In a counseling situation, one father asked if I would talk to his son. It seemed that every time the boy came to the father's new home to eat, he would vomit, even at the table. The father said every effort was made to get the boy to stop, but to no avail. Everyone in the new home loved the boy, leaving the father puzzled by his son's behavior. When the boy came to me his feet barely touched the floor as he sat in the chair. He was the cutest of eight year olds. After talking with him and with the custodial mother, and after much research, particularly in Dr. Archibald Hart's book, *Children and Divorce*, I thought the boy was suffering from severe anxiety. Each time he went to the step-family's home, he became frightened and sick. The young boy had thought that to love the new family, he would have to stop loving his mother. This unspoken conflict caused anxiety. Anxiety affects the gastrointestinal track; nausea, vomiting, and diarrhea are common symptoms. When the father realized that the discipline he gave the boy for his behavior only added to the anxiety, he stopped. I recommended that he not push his son to go to the new house. Instead, I suggested that they should meet on neutral ground and that the father should continually reinforce his love for his son. After months of reinforcement the child was reassured of his father's love, and again trusted his father. Eventually, he could go the new home without vomiting because he no longer felt he had to relinquish his love for his mother.

We are worn out, there is no rest for us...

Even in the midst of turmoil, children try to maintain loyalty to each parent, though it is difficult to do. Some kids just give up and say that they can't really be loyal. There are simply too many players to keep track of as they decide who will have their loyalty: father, step-father, mother, step-mother, step-brothers, step-sisters, half-brothers, half-sisters, and

new grandparents. The confusion produces a para-
lyzing helplessness. Thoughts of helplessness
become overwhelming. It seems that nothing comes
easy to the single-parent child. Everything comes to
him through great sacrifice. Relationships with family, grandparents, aunts, and uncles, just do not come
as easily as they once did. Someone always seems
to get hurt. Oh, the frustration of it all. The child is
worn out from trying to please everyone.

Our houses to aliens...

At the CHIPS headquarters in Lima, New York,
in the late 1980's, we had a CHIPS club for single-parent children. We sent club members a mailing on a
monthly basis to give them encouragement. The
newsletter featured teachings applicable to the lives
of single-parent children. We designated various children as the "CHIP of the Month" and included their
stories in the newsletter. But our mailing list could
not keep up with the address changes. The single
parents' constant hunt for a better home with more
space, lower rent, and a better location had the members constantly on the move. The home's role is to
provide a stable place, with a constant, loving atmos-
phere where people can grow and mature in a safe
place. In the single-parent household, with finances
fluctuating and jobs being difficult to find and hold,
the child is moved from a place of stability to one of
instability. This not only results in losing a familiar
shelter, but in a changing of neighborhoods and the
loss of valued playmates and classmates.

Playmates are important to children. Parents
who are experiencing alienation of different degrees
usually have a few people, whether family or friends,

to cling to in the midst of divorce. Children have the same needs for friendships to help them cope with their changing life scenario. The time during and following divorce is crucial time for the children to remain in contact with good friends. At this point in the attempt to make friends, many single-parent children befriend other wounded children who are acting rebellious in response to their situation. With all the loss and hurt they have experienced, the children have unresolved anger and bitterness within themselves. Connecting with others who have the same problem seems easy and is natural. The need to be accepted is especially applicable at this time, so any friend will do. But, the wounded children become difficult to befriend. Their very countenances change. Then good kids stay away from them just at a point when they truly need good friends. The enemy of our soul takes advantage of the moment.

We have become orphans without a father... Our mothers are like widows.

The heartache of losing a father truly can be heard in this verse. Having grown up in a home where my dad was my hero, I can only imagine the feeling of such heartache. As a child, if I even imagined my dad dying or leaving I would quickly try to erase the thought. I could not handle it. In a single-parent child's life, there is a great increase in his sense of vulnerability. We can liken it to having the very roof of our home being ripped off in the middle of a storm, causing irrevocable damage to the things within. The one who was to be the protector has gone. The children feel a tremendous sense of abandonment. The child feels that the divorce is actually his parents abandoning him. If children are to grow healthy in the midst of divorce, parents must reassure them that although the marriage is over, parenting will never be over. Children who face being *"orphans without a father"* face some heavy bombardment.

Wounded lambs are easy targets especially when the shepherd, in other words the parent, is also wounded. The lamb wounded in the valley must be carried by a strong shepherd until its strength is regained. The church must function as the hands and feet of the Good Shepherd, and we must be there to help the little ones caught in the midst of parental strife. If the church applies the wisdom of James 1:27 and helps the widow and orphan in their distress, a lot of heartache will surely be alleviated: *"This is pure and undefiled religion in the sight of our God and Father, to visit orphans and widows in their distress, and to keep oneself unstained by the world."* This verse does not apply only to literal orphans and widows; single parents and their children are the widows and orphans of today. If we, the body of Christ on the earth, can lift them out of their distress, the Lord's love through us can bring them healing.

We have submitted to Egypt and Assyria to get enough bread.

In the Word of God, the people of Egypt and Assyria were the enemies of God's people. Why would the people of Jerusalem want to let their children get their nourishment from the enemy? Their personal calamity was so great that they failed to act appropriately on behalf of the children. Turning to the enemy for bread can be interpreted to mean that the parent would sacrifice the children in order to get comfort — to try to remedy the sad situation the enemy's way. The children become lost in the process with no one trying to rescue them, and the enemy wastes no time in his pursuit of them.

It's easy to be fooled by the remedies that the enemy offers. Therefore, we need to teach our children about spiritual warfare. For the most part, children are not taught to understand spiritual warfare to protect themselves until they are in their teens. Yet, if abortion is the enemy's attack on children in the womb, there is no time to waste in instruction and preparation of our children to face him. If we don't teach them about spiritual warfare early, then the children will be lost in the crossing of the river from childhood to adolescence and be caught up in the sludge of the river bank. We must make them aware that the enemy is on the prowl to devour the young soul, especially in the context of the loss of a parent.

In my early ministry, I was guilty of being lulled to sleep by the subtlety of the enemy's attack on the family. At the dinner table my little girl would come home from school, reporting, "My friend Jennifer's mother and father are getting a divorce." My response might have been, "Oh, that's a shame. Pass the ketchup," or "That's too bad. I knew that was coming." Was the Lord directing my Christian daughter to come home with a report that a family was under attack, facing divorce? I don't believe in coincidence or the apathy of God, so I wonder about the significance of my child's report. What would I have done if she had come home and said, "Dad, the house across the street is burning, and I think the family is still inside?" Would my responses have been the same? No! I would have acted immediately. As Christians, we must realize that we do *"not war against flesh and blood but against principalities and powers of darkness*" (Ephesians 6:12). I now see that apathy among Christians toward families in trouble smacks of our enemy's involvement. I've come to the awareness that when there is the loss of a parent through divorce or death that the enemy is wrestling for the souls of each individual.

When my daughter reports a similar circumstance today, I tell her to intercede for the children, and we pray for the family. If the little ones need a home to come to, ours is open. We recognize the enemy's tactics, and we are not willing for any to perish. We don't want to sit around eating hot dogs while families are destroyed. Passivity on the part of the people of God pushes the parents and children to go to Egypt and Assyria for bread when the bread that they need is the Bread of Life, Jesus Christ. We, His people, are those who should be offering the Bread of Life to the little ones. We must offer them the true Bread so that they need not turn to Egypt and Assyria to get their bread. So please, pass the Bread.

Our fathers sinned, and are no more...

In many of the battles that occur during and after divorce, we find that tremendous power struggles take place over children. Sometimes parents believe that their only option in the battle is to influence the children's relationship with the other parent. This can undermine the other parent's function in the lives of the children. If the child has to witness a heart-wrenching battle between his parents, he may struggle with similar destructive behavior for generations. Abusers beget abusers, divorce begets divorce, and the sin of the family stays alive. Children may think that their lives are ruined because of their parents' mistakes. The only way the sinful pattern is broken is in and through the blood of Jesus Christ.

It is easy to take sides as single parents relate their stories with great emotion. I truly want to be sensitive and fair to both individuals of the crisis of divorce. I want to listen to each person. I don't want to be biased. However, I have observed that some women are extremely critical of their ex-spouses. Since women are usually the custodial parents, this attitude can have a powerful impact on the children. Because of experiencing so much hurt, the custodial parent may truly believe that the other parent can do nothing right. That belief can seem to make the distancing of the other parent be a way of protecting the child. But it ends up being another way of keeping the child hurt and struggling with feelings of abandonment. A child in a divorce heals most quickly when his relationships with both parents are nurtured. Mothers, as the primary custodial parents, must be careful to evaluate their motives and actions toward their former husbands as God would want them to. The woman must resist the temptation to make her children's father pay for his mistakes by not being allowed to father.

A frequent outcome of divorce is that the man is vilified and ostracized, and ultimately eliminated from fathering. Fathers in the throws of divorce have a very hard time fathering. After divorce, many fathers lose their children, willingly or unwillingly, because of hostility between the parents, guilt over their own actions, or as a result of the struggle to build a new life. This loss of contact with the father only adds to the sense of loss that the child already experiences. There are those men who truly would like to have an active part in the rearing of the children but are denied by the courts or by the mother. As I have said before, the majority who come to CHIPS seminars are custodial parents, and most of those are women. My heart aches for the men who need so much to hear of the Lord's love for them. I wonder where they are going to receive comfort from.

Many men to whom I've talked only feel worthy enough to send money — not to try to maintain a relationship with their kids. They have been shut out of all other activities. One father remarked, "Tony, I wanted children for more than the reason of supporting them; I wanted to father." Our gut level response to such a comment might be "Well, then stay married." I wish it were that simple for people to restore their damaged hearts and to learn to love again. True, in some cases a man or a woman, either by writs of protection or other court orders, is purposely kept away from his or her children. In these situations I understand the need for distancing of the children from their parent, but that's not necessary or appropriate in most cases. The majority of estranged parents are deceived and maneuvered out the door of a relationship with their children.

It is we who have borne their iniquities...

One young man came to me with his unsaved, noncustodial father at the request of his saved mother. The young man was quitting school the next day; he was failing every subject. He had scabs in his nose from doing speed and cocaine. I shared my heart and the love of Jesus with the two of them, and as they left my house I told the boy that I would pray for him and that "I pray hard." I expected a miracle.

The mighty hand of God moved that day, and the young man chose not to do drugs the next day for the first time in a year. He was back in my home within the week for more counseling. He remained open to the Holy Spirit's work and God cleaned him up supernaturally. As we talked, the boy revealed to me that the first time he lit up a joint was the day his father left home. "I remember thinking, 'If they are going to destroy their lives, I'll destroy mine'," he said. The destruction of his young life began that day! His life was destined for ruin.

He felt that his parents' sin had given him sufficient reason for destroying his own potential for success. During the course of this single-parent child's healing, he asked the Lord to forgive him for wanting to ruin his life. Repentance came; he asked the Lord for new life; and he received Jesus Christ into his life.

You see, in Christ, there is hope. Children come to life on earth *through* parents, but not *from* them. When a baby is born, the Lord has a plan. The Lord Jesus has a destiny for each life. All of the interactions of earthly life *when submitted to His hand* will work out for the good. The Lord says:

> *"A voice is heard in Ramah, lamentation and bitter weeping. Rachel is weeping for her children; she refuses to be comforted for her children because they are no more." Thus says the Lord, "Restrain your voice from weeping, and your eyes from tears; for your work*

shall be rewarded, "declares the Lord, "And they shall return from the land of the enemy. And there is hope for your future," declares the Lord, "And your children shall return to their own territory."
(Jeremiah 31:15-17)

Though we as parents sin, our children need not be bound. They can be set free through Jesus Christ.

Chapter Five

HOPE IN GOD

In reviewing the Book of Lamentations, I am so amazed at how well it expresses God's under-standing of people who are caught in calamity. There was great devastation with the collapse of the outer walls of Jerusalem and the destruction of the temple when the Babylonians attacked Israel. People lost all their possessions, and their place of worship was lev-eled to the ground. Pain, confusion, and tremendous heartache impacted the people within the confines of the city walls. When I first started to study Lamenta-tions, I only knew one verse about the faithfulness of the Lord from singing the hymn, "Great Is Thy Faith-fulness:"

"This I recall to my mind,
Therefore I have hope.
The Lord's lovingkindnesses indeed never cease,
For His compassion never fails.
They are new every morning;
Great is Thy faithfulness."
(Lamentations 3: 21 - 23)

71

My paraphrase for single parents:

> *I must remember this*
> *For I cling to God's salvation.*
> *The Lord's love is endless;*
> *His caring heart will always reach out to us.*
> *Every day is a new start.*
> *I choose to begin again with God,*
> *Who is a faithful Father.*

Today the great message of the book of Lamentations has more meaning to me than ever before.

To keep himself from becoming disheartened, Jeremiah, the author of Lamentations, had to recall the faithfulness of God in the midst of calamity. You too must recall how, in times past, you have been upheld by God's love and that He will never leave you or forsake you. His faithfulness is consistently there to hold on to. In the worst of times, when it seems as if your faith is gone, you must cling to His Word, which declares His faithfulness.

I have heard it said that when you can't see His plan or the touch of His hand, you can trust His heart. In the worst pain of my family's life, when we lost our beloved son James in 1992, my wife cried out to our dear friend Sylvia Evans, founder of Creative Word Ministries and a great Bible teacher. She said "Sylvia, I don't think I have enough faith to go through this." Sylvia's reply was so comforting: "Just hold onto *the Faith*; let those of us around you who still have faith help bring you through day by day." Faith is sometimes misconstrued just to be the kind of faith that achieves miracles — the kind that parts the sea and raises the dead and causes the lame to jump. Achieving faith occurs when God shows up and changes the circumstances through the believer or otherwise sovereignly intervenes.

Faith to achieve miracles is often the only kind of faith we consider. It is powerful, and it is available to all who believe. In Hebrews 11, we read of the great and mighty men and women of God who have their names etched in the pages of God's incredible Word. I struggled in the circumstances of our son's death because this kind of achieving faith eluded me. At times, I felt faithless because I lacked the right formula or words to bring James back.

It wasn't until then that I realized that there are two kinds of faith: *achieving faith* and *enduring faith*. The heroes of the Bible listed in Hebrews 11 are not necessarily people who overcame physically — but did spiritually. Some of the Hall of Faith occupants suffered death, mocking, scourging, imprisonment, and destitution. Their trophies of grace are inscribed with the words *Enduring Faith*. In the midst of the storm when all seems lost, don't bail out; endure. Your ship may seem to be sinking but stay in the ship because it is far more dangerous to be in the troubled waters of the world amidst the sharks. The worst time to bail out is in the midst of the storm. Hold steady.

God's Word in Luke 8: 22-25 speaks of a time when the apostles were in a boat with Jesus, going to the other side of the lake. A storm arose, and the apostles panicked, turning to Jesus who was sleeping and saying, *"Can't you see we're perishing?"* Jesus replied, *"Where is your faith?"* I used to consider that to mean, "You have no faith; you need achieving faith." They thought Jesus was rebuking them, saying, "Come on now, guys; why don't you stop the storm yourselves? Do something for yourselves!"

Pastor Tony's
first youth group,
Pt. Jefferson,
Long Island

First CHIPS weekend at
Elim Bible Institute

Jesus loves the little children

CHIPS teens receive prayer

Youth ministry at
CHIPS weekend

CHIPS weekend
snapshots . . . at left,
Pastor Tony delivers
the Lord's message . . .
above and below,
group photos

75

Today, having experienced much pain, I view it from
the other side, the enduring side. I envision Jesus
waking up saying, "Where is your faith? Can't you
see I'm in the boat with you? What can harm you?
I'm with you. Just snuggle up to me, hold on, and I'll
bring you through. That's all you have to do. I don't
expect you to eliminate the storm." It was with this
in mind that I rode out my personal storm, holding
onto the Master's arm. I now have something to
recall in times of difficulty that assures me that God
is faithful and He loves me. I know my faith works in
the valley when it needs to endure.

The Bible defines faith as *"the assurance of things
hoped for, the conviction of things not seen"* (Hebrews
11:1). Hope is such an important element for successful living. We must be a people who are hope-
filled. Single parents can be stuck in hopelessness.
It seems that they can't see beyond today, are filled
with pain, and are facing problems on every side.
But you can go to the same rock of escape that David
found in I Samuel 23:28: *"Saul returned from pursuing
David, and went to meet the Philistines; therefore they called
that place the Rock of Escape."* David was being unjustly
pursued by Saul; Saul had called for David's death.
But God brought David to the rock. Our love and
faith is in Jesus Christ, who is our rock. We can
know that *"all things work together for good to them that
love God"* (Romans 8:28 KJV).

While God is "working things together for
good," ask Him for the grace to hold on until you
come to see the good that can result from the calamity. You can hope in God's grace. If you don't
remember the faithfulness of the Lord, you will lose
hope. Jeremiah knew this and recalled the good, the
wonder, and the faithfulness of the Lord. Single par-

ent, you must, too! Hope in God. Here is an acronym for hope to help you remember:

Having
Only
Positive
Expectations

To know that the Heavenly Father is *for* you and that He is filled with lovingkindness should be a thought onto which you hold. He is for you and wants to help you make it in life. You must be persuaded that nothing shall separate you from the incredible love of your heavenly Father, for His love never ceases.

The Lord's compassions never fail. He feels for His people, especially for the single parent, the widow, and the orphan. In the Book of Luke, chapter 7, verse 11, we find the Lord stopping the funeral of a single-parent child who had died. The child's mother was a widow, and he was her only son. Scripture says that when the Lord saw the single mother weeping, He felt compassion for her and said, "*Do not weep.*" Jesus touched the coffin, returned life to the boy, and gave him back to his mother. Jesus has put a face on God for us; He reveals the heart of the Father. He feels for you. He is not a heartless God. In your situation, God feels for you, too. Let Him stop the funeral possession in your life; let Him restore life to you and your loved ones.

Each day is a new day, yet sometimes the days feel like years. Take one day at a time, for His mercy is new each morning. For the single parent, the intensity of the problems of each day is great. If you're careful not to overload your day with yesterday's baggage, receiving afresh the grace and mercy of God each day, your days should not be overwhelming. When you allow problems to build up out of anger, hatred, and frustration, then the waters of your days become murky. Take a spiritual shower each morning as you shower physically. Make that a time of spiritual preparation, cleansing, and refreshing in the Holy Ghost. Let your prayer be, "Lord, wash me clean from yesterday's pain, ease my mind of all the pressures, and give me strength to address each problem according to Your purpose for my life."

GREAT IS HIS FAITHFULNESS

What is faithfulness? This concept is hard to understand, especially when you have been surrounded by unfaithfulness. It becomes hard to trust anyone when the one to whom you have totally given yourself has walked out. Single-parent families become so damaged in the area of trust. The father and mother in marriage are intended to exemplify faithfulness so that the children can comprehend the faithfulness of God. A husband who loves his wife as Christ loves the church exemplifies God's love. A women who submits to the headship of a husband as the church submits to the headship of Christ models faith to her children. When both partners are in appropriate relationship to God and to one another, the protection of God covers the family. The devastation that occurs when parents divorce results from a split in that covering, leaving the family vulnerable. Then the enemy plants distrust. Distrust impacts the life of each member of the household — especially the children. It undermines the headship of God. It targets distrust for God, giving the children the message that they can't trust God. The next logical step is to distrust people who say they love you. However, you must teach your children that imperfect parents should drive them to the perfect one.

Jesus was born of the Holy Spirit by God the Father. Thus, Jesus had a perfect parent. In the natural, Jesus had a step-father, Joseph, and His natural mother, Mary, both of whom were imperfect. We have all had imperfect parents; they are cracked images of the one parent who is perfect. The only people besides Jesus who ever had a perfect parent were Adam and Eve. They could have had it all, but they sinned. Therefore, God, because he so loved the world, sent Jesus to redeem the losses we experienced through their sin. The imperfection of our natural parents should point us to Jesus who came to point us to His perfect Father. Single-parent families who have had the image of their heavenly Father damaged by their natural parents should be challenged to seek the Father's perfection through Jesus.

Our heavenly Father has a plan for the salvation of mankind. His standard of excellence was established on the cross of Calvary. The cross signifies the incredible sacrifice our Father made to reach us — the death of His son. For each of us trapped in sin, there is hope through Jesus Christ. And there is hope through Jesus for the family hit by heartache. The family hit by heartache needs to be filled with His love and character; a transfusion from inferior blood to superior blood. We need to make a choice to follow the ways of the Father who shaped us while we were in the womb, who has a destiny for each of us. His plans unfold as we are brought into His presence by the Holy Spirit. Salvation begins the process of redemption and healing, the restoration of each of us to become all that we can be.

Such restoration is best completed within the framework of the house of God, the church. Every single parent and child should be part of a local congregation of believers. In God's house, amidst His family, the process of healing is undertaken. It will take time depending on the seriousness of the wounds. But in God's house, with His children, His servants, the best care can be given to a hurting family. In this setting you can hold fast to the cross and walk steadily through the pain, problems, and pressure. He will heal your pain and show you the solutions to the problems. He will relieve your pressure. You will learn to trust again in His love. You will find the faith to believe that, though He did not stop the storm, He will bring you through the storm.

The steps of healing will be baby-like at the beginning; at times it will seem like you hear footsteps coming up behind you, to tackle you so you can fumble the ball. In football, the receiver who often fumbles is not a very good one. Such a player concentrates more on avoiding being tackled than upon catching the ball as he is supposed to. In learning to trust God, people who have previously been hit hard can sometimes concentrate more on avoiding being hurt again than on what the Lord has set before them to accomplish. You must keep focused on your healing or it will be difficult to attain it. If you look back constantly at incidents in the past, you may miss what the Lord is doing now in your midst. Trust the Lord, even when you can't see His hand or hear His voice. Trust His heart.

You can trust his heart because it is filled with love for all of us. You may find His love particularly difficult to receive due to the fact that earthly love has hurt you. You may feel unlovable, or you may have made a decision not to love again. Love is the character trait of God that is most dominant. He is not angry, looking to destroy us, but a Creator who wants to see life in its abundance. We must never choose not to love. When all around us fails and people have turned their backs, causing us pain, we should love. We are made to love. Our hearts are designed to feel the fullness of love.

We don't want to become heartless. This life has been infected by sin. Sin challenges us at every corner to turn our backs on love. Our heavenly Father, while we were still sinful, sent His Son. He loved us through the rebellion of sin. As Jesus faced His murderers on the cross, He cried, *"Father, forgive them, they know not what they do"* (Luke 23:34). The Holy Spirit in us calls to us to have the same love.

May I share with you a letter I received from one single parent who had lost all hope. Through Christ she received victory through a most trying situation:

> **I will never forget the first time I heard about the CHIPS ministry. I was in my early twenties, a single parent, and a new convert. My son was five years old and his father was incarcerated in a maximum security prison (he is still there at this writing). My son had great difficulty socially and emotionally, and was very impulsive and hyperactive. I later discovered when he was eight that he had suffered a blow to the head, probably at birth, that resulted in a lesion in his brain which had healed. Testing was done in a desperate attempt to**

place him in an appropriate educational setting. The situation was very severe. He was diagnosed with Attention Deficit and Pervasive Developmental Disorder with learning disabilities. Before all of this came out, my son's behaviors were a mystery to me and to my new church family.

It was hard enough to fit in being a single parent, much less one with a child who had severe behavior problems. I seemed to live in constant pain, frustration, and crisis due to my son's disabilities. Well-meaning, but often emotionally troubled individuals in the church would discipline my son to the point of abuse, oftentimes without my knowledge or consent. Everyone seemed to think it was all because he lacked discipline that he behaved this way. On many occasions someone would confess to having done something inappropriate after being confronted by another person who witnessed the abuse.

I can remember feeling like a freak, often embarrassed that I was the only person in that small church that had so many problems all of the time. I became so frustrated I would go home to my small one-room apartment after church, try to put my son down for a nap, and close the door to my bathroom to scream and cry my eyes out. I couldn't figure out why God would want me, or what in the world He would do with me.

One Sunday the assistant pastor gave a few singles in the church information on an upcoming Mobilized To Serve Conference. That fall our small group traveled to Buffalo, New York. While listening to Pastor Tony Martorana speak during a service about the first single parent in the Bible, Hagar, I had an experience I will never forget. As I sat there in my chair, it seemed as though the heavens opened to me, and I actually felt the love and acceptance of God directed specifically to my situation and life experience. As the pastor spoke, I began to cry as I sensed the Holy Spirit saying in my heart and in my mind: *You see, I know all about you. I have seen you in your despair and frustration. You are not a freak. I have a plan and a purpose for your life and a provision for your son.*

For the first time I felt truly accepted as I was and had HOPE. I was in terrible emotional pain due to my own parent's divorce and years of turbulence, uncertainty, and dysfunction. I hung onto the hope that God would help me to never emotionally or physically abandon my son as I had been abandoned in many ways.

The years have been long and very hard, but without God's provision to us the summers we attended the CHIPS weekends, I am convinced we would not have made it through to today. God's grace brought us through the desert and to the well through the CHIPS ministry. I will be forever grateful to God and to Pastor Tony Martorana for being God's hand, his smiling mustached face (I'm not sure God is Italian, though)...his broken, compassionate heart...and his booming megaphone voice demanding more oil be added to the pool of pasta for us to walk in barefoot with our kids. He brought fun and joy back to our family where there was so much anger, pain, rejection, and hopelessness. I know for certain that if it were not for those weekends, my son would never have had a true glimpse of a loving father, the only one he ever saw in the years of frowns, anger and disapproval. I know that God will bring them to his memory someday and he will serve God with all that he has in spite of the years of abuse and pain. I hold those memories in my heart and trust in the faithfulness of my God. The time when Pastor Tony's son died was one of the most critical weekends for us. Although he was in shock, he ministered to us through God's grace, and I was in awe of the grace and power of God to hold him up and keep him going.

After all the years of special schools, failure, abuse, and hardship, God allowed for my son through circumstances to attend high school in our town for his senior year. He graduated this past June. It was truly a miracle. My son was the second in my family to graduate from high school. My brother was the first. It was the biggest victory of my son's life—and mine as well.

We don't know what the future holds; my son is thinking of attending community college and is now living on his own. This is very significant since when he was born, the doctors in the hospital told me he would probably never walk or talk and that I should not take him home with me. I am seeking God's will and direction for my own life and am in the process of applying to Elim Bible Institute.

Through all that has happened in this life, no one, nothing, could ever take away the love of God that came to our little family through Pastor Tony and the CHIPS ministry. We love you, Pastor Tony—you touched us with real love—HIS. Therefore I have hope and you can too; the God who made you is *faithful.*

Chapter Six

RESTORER OF THE RUINED CITY

The loss of a husband, wife, mother, or father is not a minor incident in a person's life. Furthermore, it has major impact for the future generations, even for many generations to come. No quick solution exists; one can't offer the suffering person two scriptures, one counseling appointment, and then say, "Now go home. You're all better." It takes patience, mercy, and love on the behalf of those who want to bring the Father's healing to the single-parent family. Although I have put great emphasis upon the need for the church to care for the single-parent families in our midst, I am not interested at all in making the single-parent family the "pampered pooch" of the church. Instead, I want to see them become whole in Christ, filled with integrity and spiritual vitality, and being significant contributors to the building of God's kingdom. The enemy wants to hold individuals in slavery as Egypt held the Israelites in the time of

Moses. But God wants to lead them not only out of bondage but into a promised land. God wants to refocus their lives.

THE FIRST STEP: FOCUS FORWARD

God wants single-parent families to get focused on what's ahead, on what He has planned for them. He wants to give them a vision of a future that is filled with hope. Without a vision, people wander aimlessly like nomads in a desert. Many single-parent families are without vision for their future; they are left without hope of ever seeing their release from captivity and the healing of their wounds. God's Word declares, *"Hope deferred makes the heart sick"* (Proverbs 13:12). But God says that He has a plan for them that enables them to look forward to the future with hope: *"'For I know the plans that I have for you,' declares the Lord, 'plans for welfare and not for calamity to give you a future and a hope'"* (Jeremiah 29:11).

In order to get where God wants to take you, you must first deal properly with the past, then close the door behind you and focus on the present and the future. He wants to turn your head to the work at hand. Many make the mistake of trying to walk forward while looking back. Author and speaker Lee Edsell said it beautifully on a tape I once heard: "It's like driving your car by looking in the rear view mirror, rather than looking forward out the windshield." Just imagine riding in that back seat as a child. What a scary place. Such a driver is an accident waiting to happen. Each ditch and pothole in the road has the potential to send the car out of control. No one can live in the past this way. In II Kings 4, the prophet Elisha meets a parent in trouble. Her husband has just died, and the creditor has come to take her two

sons to force them to work to pay back a debt. Here
is an example of the place of impact. The creditor is
a type of the enemy who wants to take the children
captive. But through Elisha, God was right there.
"Help, man of God" cries the woman. "What do you
have in your house?" responds Elisha. "Nothing but
a little oil," shrugs the woman. Sounds like a single-
parent house to me! The woman reveals what I call a
"nothingness mentality," a pervasive way of thinking
which focuses on what one *doesn't* have. "Go get me
a bunch of empty vessels," says the man of God.
The assignment of the Lord is given through Elisha to
the single parent, and she follows the instructions.
He wants her to pour out the little oil she has into the
empty vessels.

In the end, God filled all the vessels, the
widow sold the oil, and paid off her creditors. But
before that could occur, she had to obey one more
little instruction. Elisha said, "Before you begin to
pour, close the door behind you and your sons." In
other words, "Let's get on with what the Lord has for
your life today. In order to do that, you must stop
the interference of yesterday's painful and destructive memories." The memories you must leave
behind are those that continually stick in your head,
gaining an entrance to today through the door left
open to yesterday. They include painful memories
that continually distract your attention and sap you of
the strength you have in God. Closing the door on
painful memories does not mean that you close the
door on your former spouse's foot, or slam it in his
or her face. In other words, closing the door on
painful memories does not include deliberately injur-
ing your former spouse. Do all you can to close the
door with firmness, but with integrity. For example, if

the marriage is truly over, and there is no life left in it, you must let go of it, even though you would prefer reconciliation.

THE NEXT STEP: SURRENDER

Closing the door is the beginning of the process of healing. The next step is to move through the door marked "Surrender." When you go through the door of surrender to God's will, it's like going to the airport and passing through the security metal detector. Anything that triggers the alarm has to be looked at by the security personnel. Explosives, weapons, and bombs aren't allowed on the plane. Similarly, in the life of the single parent, there are attitudes and patterns of behavior that you cannot take with you through the door of surrender because they are ungodly and cannot coexist with God's will in your life. Ungodly fears, deeply rooted anger and hatred, bitterness and resentments, jealousy and vengeance all set off the security alarm on God's holy way. Choosing to leave these attitudes behind is an essential part of finding freedom in the Lord. A single parent who walked through the door of surrender wrote to me, saying,

> **"God did a mighty work in me, and I have not been the same at all. I feel alive! I had become so bitter and discouraged that I was pulling away from God and the church. I was experiencing so much pain. God really did what you said He would. He came to free me from being a captive. He took His probe and touched me where I was hurting and showed me truths that literally changed my thinking. Thoughts of hate and revenge don't harass me. Instead I have compassion toward my former spouse."**

Let God defuse the bombs. He is a specialist.

Although they are evil, negative feelings can become like "security blankets," appearing to provide a measure of comfort. To go without a security blanket to some children is intolerable, and yet they are often happier when they free themselves from their need for it. My youngest daughter would not let go of her "blankee" for the longest time. It was tattered and torn, but it held great value in her eyes. One day in a church we were visiting, a younger child crying in the nursery needed a blankee desperately, and my daughter yielded to our encouragement to give it up. Many single parents and children carry things like anger, vengeance, bitterness, fear, hatred, and self-destructive attitudes as a kind of security blanket that protects them from further injury, but they must say, "Enough. I lay it all at the feet of Jesus." It can be terribly frightening to let go of those destructive behaviors that masquerade as protection and to trust God and allow him to instill righteous ones. Just know this: He is trustworthy. In time, He will replace your misguided trust in the wrong attitudes and bring you to a state of maturity in the area of your weakness.

THE OUTCOME: REDEFINITION

As you surrender to God, he gives you a new outlook. You see yourself, your life, and your circumstances from the underside, but He wants to lift you up and give you the perspective from His vantage point, in the heavenly place. Literally, He wants to remake you into the very likeness of His Son Jesus. Let God redefine how you see yourself. As this transformation happens, the wounds you have suffered will be healed and will become the means by which you can heal others. The stumbling blocks that have sent you sprawling will become the very stepping stones upon which you will build. Rather than being brought down, as you surrender to God, you will be lifted up. Henrietta Mears once said, "The greatness of your power is equal to the measure of your surrender."

We see this same principle working in the lives of many people in the Bible. In Genesis we see young Joseph who became a single-parent child after his mother, Rachel, died giving birth to his brother Benjamin. His older brothers sought to destroy him and sold him into slavery. They later discovered that he had become the most powerful man in all of Egypt. Then, it was he who became their "savior." Our Father took what the enemy had meant for evil in Joseph life, and He used it for good to save both Isaac's family and the Egyptians from starvation during a famine. Just as Joseph said to his brothers, we should be able to say to the enemy and to those who have offended us, "*You meant evil against me, but God meant it for good in order to bring about this present result, to preserve many people alive*" (Genesis 50:20). So great is our God that by the very injuries we receive, He can strengthen us and enable us to bless others in their need. Joseph's life, though filled with heartache and loss, was used by God. This truth of power through surrender to God's will is not only true for Joseph's life, but also for you and the lives of your children and others who are suffering.

Renewal begins when you truly surrender your life to Jesus Christ. When you admit before God your sinful behaviors, and ask Him for forgiveness, he forgives you and gives you a new life. This new life is lived out through His Holy Spirit, who leads you to more and more truth, maturing you in your places of weakness. Then, like Paul, you will be able to say, "*We can comfort those in any trouble with the comfort we ourselves have received from God"* (II Corinthians 1:4).

There is another story in the Bible about a single-parent family. The widow that Elijah visited in I Kings 17:9-24 was a single parent, and she and her son were about to eat their last meager meal and die. The Lord led Elijah to her door to ask her for a meal. The request for water was well received, and she graciously responded, but when the prophet asked her for bread she flared, "As the Lord your God lives, can't you see I have nothing?" She was fearful of death. The Lord, through Elijah, said, "Fear not, give me something to eat first, and watch what God will do." Despite her own desperate situation, she did what the Lord required of her. Did she die as a result? No, instead the Lord multiplied what she had so that she and her son never went hungry in the midst of a great famine. She could have said, with some justification, "I can't do anything for anybody else. I've lost everything that I need for my child and myself. I'm a sole parent, and life is too tough." She broke through the nothingness mentality. As a result, her obedience became the means that God used to provide for the prophet's needs, for her needs and her child's needs. This single parent gave all single parents a tremendous example to consider and emulate. If you will focus on God and His will for you and for your children, He will be your provider, and, in the process of fellowshipping with Him, you will be lifted up. As you are lifted up, others will notice and will come to recognize that you are seated in a heavenly place with God. Therefore, rather than looking upon you as a weak creature to be pitied, others will see God's strength in you. They will be asking you to help them, and you will be able to do it. Despite your personal wounds, as great as they are, you will become a healer, just as through His woundedness Jesus became a healer. One of the many letters I have received states this so well. A single parent who attended a Single-Parent Day Seminar wrote:

> I applied the principles I learned, and there's been a miracle in me and in my family; God has blessed me with a servant's heart and is effecting change in my church. I started to obey the principles you taught. When I attended the seminar my children were in great pain. One was starting therapy at the request of the school. The other was undergoing tests due to a personality change and headaches. Both are now healing. They are healing because I cried and allowed God to heal me. And I told them Jesus was in charge, and we were going to obey him. We began by focusing outside ourselves. I explained that God wanted us to make a difference in someone's life. We prayed, we gave, we sponsored a Compassion International child. My daughter began watching a Down Syndrome baby so her mom could attend Christian aerobics. Instead of feeling sorry for ourselves at church, alone and alienated, we began looking for people who were alone, talking to them and listening to them. We have too much to offer to sit still. We are excited and renewed. I taught a third grade Sunday school class this year very grudgingly. Now though, God has blessed this class as child after child meets Jesus and begins to grow. You are so right about blocking the channels of receiving by feeling there is nothing left to give. Single-parent families are powerful in what we have to give. God uses this. What a difference in my life! May God continue to bless your ministry.

This woman walked through the door of surrender and said, "Your way Lord, not mine." Our heavenly Father wants to take from you nothing that is good for you. He takes only that which will cause you grief and pain. You can trust Him even when life brings you pain, either self-inflicted by your own sinful nature or put on you by someone else's sin. He will see you through. You are made in the image and likeness of God. Say to yourself, "My life is not over. It's just beginning because of my walk with God!"

JESUS: RESTORER OF THE RUINED CITY

The enemy wants you to despair as you languish among the ruins, but God wants to restore you. He will restore you while renewing your confidence in the value of living, in spite of any setbacks or suffering that you experience.

While we are sitting among the rubble of once-grand dreams and aspirations it seems impossible to hope for restoration. It is impossible when we look through the eyes of fear. But, thank God, we are not limited to that outlook when we know the Lord. His Word assures us: "*I will bring to [the city] health and healing, and I will heal them; and I will reveal to them an abundance of peace and truth*" (Jeremiah 33:6). We can look up to Him and cry, "*Abba, Daddy!*" (Romans 8:15). He is our dad. When we give our lives to Christ, and are obedient, He will lead us to victory. When we allow ourselves to envision our loss through the eyes of faith, then we are free to release the situation to God, permitting Him to establish His will on Earth (in our life circumstances) as it is in heaven.

The wounds that single parents and their children suffer are serious injuries. In fact, the enemy intends them to be crippling, even death-producing. So it was, also, with the wounds that Jesus suffered. The very wounds that put Him in the grave led, ultimately, to the resurrection by which He, and we in Him, gained victory over death. This is the nature of Christ. *He takes the worst and makes it the best.*

Thus, from the place of rejection or woundedness, we can rally in Christ. He is our example: *"The stone which the builders rejected, this became the chief cornerstone"* (Matthew 21:42). Jesus, who was tested by the rejection He faced from so many people, did not succumb to its pressure. He was not defeated by Peter's denial, or by the crowd's abuse, or by Herod's anger, or by the temporary alienation from God the Father that he experienced. Each one of these instances created an opportunity to increase his character and testimony. I pray, "Lord, help us be as true as Jesus was, so that our dashed hopes become hope-filled testimonies to the glory of God." Our strength in the Lord can be the same as that in Revelation 12:11: *"And they overcame [Satan] because of the blood of the Lamb and because of the word of their testimony."* The blood of the Lamb is available to us as believers now. A single parent who comes full circle in the healing process develops a powerful word of testimony to share. The loss of a spouse, or more critically of a father or a mother, is one of the major traumas of life. Encouragement from the mouth of those who have suffered this same loss is a powerful tool in the hands of God. Words of encouragement will do wonders for those who are wounded. To triumph through one of life's major threats is the mark of a champion, and we are more than champions, *"more than conquerors"* through Jesus (Romans 8:37 NIV).

Several summers ago while teaching in Miami, Florida, I had a kidney-stone attack. It came after speaking some fifteen times in one week of camp to Spanish-speaking children through an interpreter. The week had been one of faith and power, and then in a moment, I was on my knees, in pain. It felt like I was giving birth to an elephant. After such a mighty week, I was crawling and moaning in the back seat of the car.

The pain was excruciating. The pastor's daughter took me to the hospital. They hooked me up to an IV bottle, and the pain subsided. It was awful. After being released from the hospital free of pain, but not knowing whether or not the stone had passed, I left Florida for Rochester, New York. I missed my connection in Atlanta, Georgia, and had to stay overnight in a hotel, wondering if the awful pain would return.

When I finally arrived home, I consulted my family doctor. I told him of the pain the stone had caused, and its intensity. He told me that an aneurysm in the brain, massive heart failure, and the passing of a kidney stone were the three most severe types of pain that a person can experience. The doctor said that on a scale of one to ten, labor pains being a ten, a kidney stone is a twelve! When I thought about what I had been through, I said to the Lord, "That was incredibly tough, but I withstood one of the worst pains, and thank you, God, I made it." Likewise, my dear single parent, you have withstood one of the toughest heartaches of life. You were knocked down, but it's over, and it's time to get up. You are a *winner* through Christ Jesus.

I know that in the midst of the pain it might seem that all is ruined. You may feel as though you have always had to suffer. You had put your hopes for love and protection in a man or woman, and your dreams came tumbling down around you. What's the answer? Some people think that all they need to do is go find another more compatible mate and that a new relationship will end the search for peace and love. In John 4, we read that a woman of Samaria who came to the well to quench her thirst felt like that. At the well, she met a man, Jesus, who was, and still is, the ultimate thirst quencher, and He asked her for a drink. She didn't realize that Jesus could satisfy her longings, so she didn't ask him for a drink. He said to her, *"If you knew the gift of God, and who it is that says to you, 'Give Me a drink,' you would have asked Him, and He would have given you living water"* (John 4:10). This woman sought to satisfy her natural thirst and did not realize her true need to meet the ultimate fulfiller. She eventually asked for a drink. Then the Lord told her, *"Go, call your husband." "I have no husband,"* she replied. The Lord, knowing her situation, replied: *"You have well said, 'I have no husband'; for you have had five husbands; and the one whom you now have is not your husband; this you have said truly"* (John 4:17).

Five husbands? What was she looking for in a man? In this present day, we could see her, maybe, with Sam, the first one, who in high school had a nice car, but in time, when it rusted, so had the attraction between them. Then there was Ted; he had a job, but he didn't make enough. So long! Harry had lots of money, but he was spoiled by his parents. Mario owned an accounting business and worked hard for his money, but he never was home. Bill was a family man, but he loved to watch the horse races. Good-bye. I believe the Lord would say to her, "Sister, the answer is not in Sam, Ted, Harry, Mario, or Bill. What you need is in Me, Jesus, and I'm offering myself to you as Living Water."

How many times must we be faced with the decision to accept His love? Jesus is our rock and fortress, our strong tower in whom we can trust. You can look to be fulfilled in the natural, but without Jesus you will never be satisfied. Those who marry may look to the family as their source of strength and protection. But, the thousands of single parents whose families have fractured will be the first to say, "You can't put all your hopes and dreams in the marriage basket, either." Put your hope in the real protector.

Zechariah prophesied that some day the city of Jerusalem and the temple would no longer need walls to protect it; the Lord was going to transform that ruined city of Jerusalem into a thriving center of life again, with one major difference: He would be the protector, surrounding it and filling it with Himself: *"Jerusalem will be inhabited without walls, because of the multitude of men and cattle in it. For I will be a wall of fire around her, and I will be the glory in her midst"* (Zechariah 2:4 -5) (see Illustration #3 on page 35). In Zechariah 1:16, the Lord promised: *"I will return to Jerusalem with compassion; My house will be built in it."*

Protection does not mean to simply put walls around the city. The Father is aware that only He can defend the temple. Likewise to place people in the marriage structure is not sufficient protection for the family members. We cannot build our lives on marriage as the ultimate place of protection, any more than we can protect the temple by building walls of mortar and clay around it. The Father knows this, and that's why He sent His Son, Jesus Christ. Some members of our society want to build a stronger society on strong families; they are close to being right, but building our lives on nothing less than Jesus Christ and His righteousness is the true strong foundation. Jesus said, *"Therefore every one who hears these words of Mine and acts upon them, may be compared to a wise man, who built his house upon the rock...the floods came, and the winds blew...and yet it did not fall..."* (Matthew 7:24-25). The family must be protected by the Lord Himself. He is the only one who can protect and maintain each individual. Each individual who is strong in the Lord keeps the wall of fire about the home.

To have enjoyed a positive and cherished relationship and then to have lost it, or to not have had it when you should have can produce what seems like irreparable emotional damage in your life. The world will not be shocked if you are filled with bitterness, anger, or self-pity. This response is "only natural." But is this any reason to close yourself in with these destructive feelings when God has offered a better alternative? Consider the story of Hagar and Ishmael in Genesis 21:9-20. After Ishmael was caught mocking Isaac, Ishmael and his mother, Hagar, were told to leave the comfort and riches of Abraham's home. The only provisions Abraham gave them was enough bread and water to last a short time. After the bread and the water were used up, both mother and child were left to die, wandering in the wilderness.

Hagar was ready to give up her life as well as the life of her son. As they sat apart from one another weeping, God heard the lad crying. He sent an angel with a message to Hagar. "What's the matter with you, Hagar?" the angel asked. Before she had time to answer, the angel said, "Fear not." The angel identified fear — the same fear that drove Elijah into the wilderness (see I Kings 19).

In order to receive and retain a new vision from the Lord, it is so important not to fear. One single parent put it so well in a letter she wrote to me:

> *FEAR*...that's the spirit that overtakes us when
> we're suddenly alone...Fears for our children's
> protection from all the terrible things that lurk
> out there in the vague beyond. Tell them not to
> be afraid. God is bigger than all of our circum-
> stances. He was not surprised when the separa-
> tion and divorce occurred. He did not go back
> to the drawing board! So what if our kids' lives
> are not the picture-perfect American dream?
> God is bigger. The greatest gift we can give our
> children at this time is not protection from life
> or a relationship with the ex, or insulation from
> difficulty, but a demonstration of how to go
> through it with God by our side. In this is
> tremendous potential. With God, our kids can
> develop strong character and compassion for
> other hurting people — *with God.* We model
> that for them when we forgive, when we work
> with the ex-spouse in whatever way God shows
> us, and when we're transparent and open about
> our hurts.

Fear is the wrong emotional response. Fear can
blind a person and cause tremendous loss of direction. The woman writing the letter was a divorced
mother of two daughters. She wrote after attending a
weekend conference where she heard me talking
about forgiving the ex-spouse. She started her letter
by saying:

> "I wanted to jump out of my seat and shout,
> 'Listen to this man! He is so right on with this
> and even though it goes against everything
> you're feeling right now, *you must do it.* It's

God's command. The result will be not merely survival, but blessing beyond belief!'"

In our own power, the best we can do is attempt to free ourselves of things that hurt us, often by shutting ourselves off from people or by giving up on life as Hagar was about to do. This is not God's best. As Jesus began his earthly ministry, he stood up on a Sabbath morning and declared that He was the one who had come to fulfill the words of Isaiah 61:

> *"to comfort all who mourn, and provide for those who grieve in Zion — to bestow on them a crown of beauty instead of ashes, the oil of gladness instead of mourning, and a garment of praise instead of a spirit of despair. They will be called oaks of righteousness, a planting of the Lord for the display of his splendor. They will rebuild the ancient ruins and restore the places long devastated; they will renew the ruined cities"* (Isaiah 61:2 - 4).

Truly, what is impossible for man is possible with God — in Christ. In God we have a choice. Will we seek comfort in self-pity because we are *ruined?* Or will we accept the glorious victory our Lord offers and be renewed?

Let's talk about rebuilding. First the foundation must be laid. I trust you get the message that our foundation is laid through a personal relationship with Christ Jesus. In 1997, the town of Jarrell, Texas, was devastated by a forceful tornado with incredible winds of 160 miles per hour. While watching the news footage, I saw that blocks of homes were totally blown away. In some instances all that was left was debris spread across an area where a home once stood. I thought: *"These poor people don't even know where their homes are."* Yet for some, in the midst of the devastation stood *the foundation* of the house they had lost: a place to rebuild upon. When intense heartache comes to a life, it has the power to blow you away. The power of the pain can make you feel as though a tornado has come through your heart. A spiritual base is the most important foundation you can have when it comes to issues of the heart. It gives you the ability to hold onto faith no matter what comes your way and to know that the Lord loves you and will bring you through. With a true spiritual foundation you have the ability to claim the enduring faith available in Christ to endure without fear overtaking you. Hagar, in her distress, settled for death. But the angel broke in and shared the Word of the Lord, *"Arise, Hagar, and take your child by the hand"* (Genesis 21:18). Today, the angel would say, "Get up, single parent, life is not over for you or your child. Stop your limping; God's got a bigger vision for you."

Life in Christ is bigger than your circumstances. What joy must have filled Hagar and Ishmael's hearts as they were lifted from the devastation of their loss. God was not finished with them; He opened Hagar's eyes to see a well. Were her eyes closed? No, her eyes were open in the natural, but she could not see the plan of God. So many single parents are in this condition: eyes open but with no vision. *"Where there is no vision, the people perish"* (Proverbs 29:18 KJV).

As Hagar and Ishmael did, many single parents lose their forward movement in the face of divorce or the death of a spouse, and begin wandering aimlessly like nomads in the desert. The goodness of the Lord restored Hagar's vision, and she saw God's provision for her salvation. There was refreshment at last for this single-parent family. The Lord is no respecter of persons; what was available to Hagar and her son is also available to you and your family. He is our hope when we are hopeless.

Mentally, the single parent has a real challenge to face. The single parent needs to break out of the rut of thinking that the fullness of life was yesterday. The Lord is able to give new vision and purpose to a life that He has destined to bring glory to Himself. Single parents must make a conscious effort to enlarge their thinking to think God thoughts that will catapult them onto God's new path. The mind is a fertile field; it will grow that which is planted in it. Rely on yesterday's labor, and before too long you'll have a garden of weeds. Daily cultivation and systematic feeding with the sun and rain of the Lord will give you a victory garden.

The same is true of your mental outlook on life. You're being deceived if you're expecting something fresh to grow in your life today when you can only talk about what "used to be." May I make some recommendations to you to help you along your way? Read the Bible on a consistent basis. Allow the Holy Scriptures to dominate your mind, and allow your mind to be the very richest of soil for biblical seed. Select just one scripture per week or month that has significance for you, memorize it, and meditate on it. When thoughts of defeat and fear come, recall the verse and speak it aloud. If you can take control of what you allow to enter your mind, fighting the temptation to ponder the negative, you will be well on your way to healing and victory. There are so many positive life-building books on the bookshelves today. Keep one at your night table to read before retiring.

If you are struggling with finances, learn to be obedient to God's word about tithing. When Abraham returned from a battle in which God had given him a great victory, he gave one tenth of the spoils to Melchizedek, whom the Bible calls "priest of God Most High," in gratitude to the Lord (see Genesis 14:17-20). When you show God that you trust Him and truly do love Him with *all* your mind, heart, and strength by being obedient in the realm of tithing, He will pour out a blessing upon you:

> *"Bring the whole tithe into the storehouse, that there may be food in my house. Test me in this, says the Lord Almighty, and see if I will not throw open the floodgates of heaven and pour out so much blessing that you will not have room enough for it."*
> (Malachi 3:10 NIV)

One faithful single-parent contributor to CHIPS who used to have a real struggle with finances and with her job wrote:

> **Dear Friends at CHIPS,**
> I've been wanting to share all of this year's victories. A big one is a large raise at work as well as faithfulness, at last, on my former husband's part with his timely child-support payments. I only had about $10-$20 last summer when I wrote my seed-faith check for $7.50. Since then I have tithed faithfully and wow! has God ever blessed. Now I can give even more back to Him! CHIPS was a real turning point for me in bringing about all of this.

This sister responded to God in obedience at a crossroad and God brought victory.

Another way to move on is to get some additional schooling. This change can be the very thing you need in order to break out of your rut. On several occasions, I've sat in on college courses that were of interest to me. In doing so, I was able to interact with younger students and share my faith, as well as be stimulated in my own thinking. We should always be increasing our knowledge in some form through education. Single parents can take courses in their local schools that will help them to advance in the work force. Do not be satisfied with the bottom of the ladder. You can move toward the top by showing a desire to improve, and be a blessing to your employer in the meantime. Some single parents I know have been motivated to enter fulltime schooling. From learning to be a truck driver to becoming a registered nurse, single parents who want more for themselves and their children go out on the limb — for the best fruit is on the ends of the branches.

THE CHURCH AS THE WORLD'S TRAUMA UNIT
The loneliness, fear, rejection, and abuse that are caused by divorce don't just fade away. With the kinds of wounds you have suffered as a single parent, you may discover that some people, even those in the church, treat you as though you should be able to just spring back and be emotionally and spiritually healthy immediately. However, the wounds you have received will not heal with a simple Band-Aid. You are like a victim of a major earthquake. Everything that used to make you feel secure has turned to rubble, and you have been buried by it. You feel like you have been crushed. There is a terrible paralysis that sets in after the shock hits you. Emotionally, you have been severely battered and lacerated. A smile and a cliché won't fix what's wrong. You need tender but persis-

tent, loving care for yourself and, don't forget, for your children.

Have you ever known people who have suffered severe physical trauma, perhaps from an automobile accident, a serious fall, or a sports injury, and experienced paralysis because of it? The doctor doesn't slap them on the back, and tell them to get well. Nor does he tell them their life is effectively over and that they should forget getting back to normal. Most likely, along with showing compassion and offering verbal encouragement, he'll place them in the care of a physical therapist who will work with them on a daily basis. At first, they'll work on trying to get one finger to move and gradually work toward getting the other parts of the body to move again. It's a slow, often tedious process. But without such therapy the healing just won't happen.

Perhaps, like other single parents, you have reached out for support from people in the church, but found a lack of sensitivity and understanding that only increased your pain and fear — especially the fear of rejection. Now, rather than being in the center of the flock where you can be helped, you are hiding in a cave of fear — right where the enemy wants you! Now I must admonish you. We can recognize that the church has not really come to grips with the problems of single parents in its midst, but blaming the church is not going to help you. If you have been driven away to the outskirts of the flock and the enemy comes *"seeking whom he may devour"* (I Peter 5:8), you are the one who will be gobbled up. And if your preoccupation with your own hurts causes you to neglect your children's needs, they will perish along with you.

It's true that the church should be seeking to draw you to its center — not after you are through your distress, but while you are still in it. But if church members fail in their responsibility, that doesn't mean you have reason to lie down and die. If the flock won't draw you to its center, then you need to place yourself there: become actively involved in the life of the church community; attend services regularly so that you may be built up in your faith; offer to serve in some capacity to help you get your focus off your own needs.

On a recent call-in program on a Christian radio station, listeners were invited to share their insights concerning various types of abuse, including child abuse, spouse abuse, etc. One woman demonstrated her understanding of the principle I'm trying to stress here. She had gone to a church trying to find some-one who could counsel her as she sought to deal with her problems as an abused woman and single parent. Sadly, there was no one capable of understanding what she had been through. But did she turn away from the church? No, she not only hung in there, but she went to college, got a degree in counseling and presented herself to the pastor as a volunteer coun-selor for people with problems like hers. The victim became a victor and is now helping other victims gain victory in their lives, too. You may think of this caller as an exceptional woman, but when you let God have your problems you discover that He is an exceptional God, and He can enable you to do exceptional things.

Chapter Seven

THE ROLE OF THE CHURCH

Historically, the church has focused on the preservation of the institution of marriage, to keep it from breaking apart and to keep it healthy and "normal." Obviously we want to see strong marriages. But, we must not get so fixated on the institution that we are not adequately aware of the individuals within it who are caught in the middle of marriages that have been attacked. Some are inclined to view separation, divorce, and having a child before getting married, as we view death. Just as we don't keep trying to help someone after he has died, so the family that has undergone one of these "abnormal" experiences is often abandoned. The intense ministry that was offered by the church before the "death" is terminated.

Is any institution more valuable than the individual members of it? Certainly not from God's perspective. When the church turns away from those who have suffered the trauma of a family breakup, in a instant we can push them into Satan's hands. Each member of the family that is caught in the battle becomes wounded. Men, women, and especially children, suffer severe heartache. We must not abandon those caught in the battle when they are most vulnerable to being taken captive.

Even a cursory look at the statistics presented in Chapter One on the many varieties of single-parent families should convince us of the magnitude of the attack that the enemy has hurled against families in America and throughout the world. In response to this attack, the church is being called to go on the offensive by means of intercession and ministry to single-parent families as it has never been provided before. The attack is fierce, but God has said, "*When the enemy shall come in like a flood, the Spirit of the Lord shall lift up a standard against him*" (Isaiah 59:19 KJV).

I believe the mission of the church is twofold: first, we must focus and strengthen all the homes that belong to the household of faith so that they are able to withstand the forces of evil. Every father, mother, and child must understand the viciousness of the attack and the pain it can cause for generations. Second, the church must insure that even if a marriage breaks, the souls will still be loved and cared for by the body of Christ.

There are men, women, and multitudes of children who have suffered the devastation of divorce or the death of a spouse or parent and have broken hearts. It is important to note that divorce itself does not hold them captive, but the choices they make following divorce do. The situation is much like an earthquake — the earthquake doesn't kill the people; the buildings that fall down on the people afterwards do.

The following verses lay out the principles for the role of the church in the release of the single-parent family from the enemy's control:

James 1:27:
> *This is pure and undefiled religion in the sight of our God and Father, to visit orphans and widows in their distress...*

Isaiah 61:1-4:
> *The Spirit of the Lord God is upon me because the Lord has anointed me to bring good news to the afflicted; He has sent me to bind up the brokenhearted, to proclaim liberty to captives and freedom to prisoners; to proclaim the favorable year of the Lord and the day of vengeance of our God; to comfort all who mourn, and grant those who mourn in Zion, giving them a garland instead of ashes, the oil of gladness instead of mourning, and the mantle of praise instead of a spirit of fainting. So they will be called oaks of righteousness, the planting of the Lord that He may be glorified. Then they will rebuild the ancient ruins. They will raise up the former devastations; And they will repair the ruined cities, the desolations of many generations.*

Psalm 147:3:
> *He heals the brokenhearted and binds up their wounds.*

NOT THE UNPARDONABLE SIN

As I began this ministry, the people of the church, including the church leaders, were at a loss as to what they could do to minister to the children

of single-parent homes. Their bewilderment wasn't
malicious in nature — it was just a lack of sensitivity.
It seemed that some thought, "God hates divorce.
We don't condone divorce so how can we possibly
help those caught in it and bring healing to them?
Helping them might seem as though we approve of
what they've done. We can help people through any
kind of sin as long as they are married." To many in
the church, it was as if divorce were the unpardonable sin even though the Bible does not support this
notion.

Another situation that God does not consider
to be the "unpardonable sin" is being an unwed
mother. The church seeks to persuade unmarried
girls and women who become pregnant not to abort
their babies. Many Christians have established crisis
pregnancy centers to reach out to unwed mothers.
But then what do we do? Do we reject them because
they are unwed mothers? Or do we offer to come
alongside them, to present a safe place in God's family? Can we be there for them as they face the struggles of single parenting? These women then need to
be taken into the body of Christ to receive on-going
ministry and fellowship.

As strange as it may sound, it seems there has
been *too much* emphasis on the family — on the "normal" family as many churches defined it: Mom and
Dad, 2.3 kids, a dog, a cat, and a house in suburbia.
The church put so much emphasis on protecting the
healthy family that it was not prepared to deal with
the families whose health had completely failed —
more precisely and critically, with the *individuals* from
such families. My heart was breaking as I saw young
people from single-parent homes turning to the world

for solace, comfort, and acceptance. All the support and guidance that the church should have been providing was not being offered because they were unprepared to provide it, or were even incapable of providing it. I cried out to God the Father to help the children, and I believe He answered me. I knew Jesus wanted to heal them while they were young.

In the book of Mark, we find Jesus speaking specifically about divorce (see Mark 10:2-12). He truly hated divorce. He knew that in the audience there were people who had been impacted by divorce, that the issue was relevant to that society. Do you think the people listening to His message needed to hear it? He wasn't speaking just to educate the priests and the happy couples. The verse immediately following verse 12 says that the people *"began bringing children to Him, so that He might touch them; and the disciples rebuked them"* (Mark 10:13). What was going on here? It is possible that the flow of these verses in Mark 10 is simply coincidental. It is also possible that the Lord intended there to be a connection between verses 2 through 12 and verses 13 through 16. The paragraph break between them was added by translators of the Bible; it is not part of the original. Who would you expect to approach Jesus immediately following His message on divorce? If someone preaches on physical healing, who do you suppose would approach him afterwards? The physically ill would respond, and he would pray with them. When Jesus preached about divorce, the conviction must have been powerful. Who responded to Jesus' words? The people who were affected by it. These single parents of Biblical times well knew, as do single parents today, that their children had been wounded, and they wanted to bring them to Jesus so that He could minister to them. He was more than willing to do so because He understood their pain.

But how could the disciples have been so heartless? What kind of ministers were they? I never could understand why the apostles rebuked the children until the Lord opened my eyes. One could interpret these verses to mean that the apostles, hearing how Jesus hated divorce, assumed he wanted nothing to do with the people who were caught in it, including the children. But Jesus saw this misinterpretation. He was indignant and said to apostles, *"Permit the children to come to Me; do not hinder them; for the kingdom of God belongs to such as these"* (Mark 10:14). Jesus raised His voice in disgust to say to His followers, "Fellows, if you don't receive little ones such as these, you've missed the whole point." Mark reports that Jesus then took these little ones *"in His arms and began blessing them, laying His hands upon them"* (Mark 10:16). Whenever Jesus lays His hands on someone in the scripture, someone gets healed. What were these children's problems? They weren't suffering from physical illnesses but from broken hearts.

I believe CHIPS was born to remove the hindrances that are in the way of children receiving the Lord's touch in the midst of their heartache. Sometimes the hindrances are circumstances, and sometimes they are grown-up people interfering, blocking the children's way to Jesus. Let the people of God not make the same error that the disciples did in Mark 10.

WOUNDED LAMBS BECOME LOST SHEEP

If the church doesn't help the wounded individuals, they will be lost to the enemy. It is in the

112

place of impact, when the protective wall of marriage is destroyed, that the enemy begins to delude the members of the family. To the husband, he whispers, "Go out and get drunk. You've blown it now. What's the use of trying anymore? Find another woman." He looks to impose fear on the wife, saying, "You are lost now. You have been rejected. You have nobody to defend you and take care of you. You're alone. No one will help you meet your needs. You might as well give up. Your situation is hopeless." And to the children who are confused and, for the most part, taken by surprise, he whispers, "Your parents have really messed up your life. If they're going to destroy their lives, go destroy yours. Show them that you're not going to let their divorce or battles affect you! Nothing really matters anymore anyway. Maybe you'll find something worthwhile in drugs, in sex, or in the excitement of the streets." In their vulnerability, the children are in great need of help. Kids today are facing adult problems at a very young age, and these problems must be ministered to for the current generation's sake and for that of the next generation. The problems faced are so severe that the children could be caught and trapped in a lifetime of misery.

In their pain and their limited strength, single parents and their children seek support from whatever source *will* help. However, the enemy offers false help which turns the wounded into captives. The children, especially, buy into the false help, causing even more injury, and manifest their woundedness in behavior that can appear inappropriate to others. For example, we are often quick to label a single-parent child as "a rebel." Children from single-parent homes don't necessarily dress neatly. The parent has little time to press clothes or keep up with the wash. The children don't act properly, and are often not very trusting. The enemy has worked overtime to strike them down. They are diagnosed with Attention Deficit Disorder or sent for psychiatric counseling, when in fact the acting out that they demonstrate is a response to the loss of a dad or mom and to a broken heart.

At one church in which I was invited to speak, the pastor's wife shared about a local family with three children. They were the most rebellious kids she had ever seen. She said, "It seems trouble follows them everywhere they go." I asked if they attended church and she said, "Sometimes." I spoke at the evening service. I shared about the Father's heart toward the widow and the orphan. After the service a woman came to me and asked if I would pray for her three boys. As I waited for them, the pastor informed me that this was the woman his wife had mentioned earlier that day. In came three scruffy, tattered and torn, dirty-faced boys who reminded me of myself as I grew up in the streets of the Bronx. I went down to meet them and was told they were 9, 7, and 5 years old. I said, "I heard you guys were having a tough time of it." I said that I knew it wasn't easy living without a father, and I bet they missed not having him around. They all nodded their heads. I told them that I didn't think they were bad kids, and that in fact, I thought they were good kids. However, the hurt inside them was because they were wounded. At this point, all three troublesome boys had tears streaming down their faces. I asked them if they had bad feelings against their

mother and father. They each nodded. I reassured
them that Jesus heard their prayers, and that I was
here to share His love with them. I asked them to
pray a prayer of forgiveness toward their parents, and
they did. I hugged them, and we stayed huddled for
ten minutes embraced in the love of the Father.
Were they rebels? No, just wounded lambs. That's
how I see so many single-parent children.

Unfortunately, though, few understand the true
cause of the children's behavior. As I travel the
country many people are happy to hear I'm dealing
with these children simply because they see them as
such a nuisance. The church pushes them to the
outskirts of the flock, where they can be easily
snatched away. Then they are wounded lambs destined to become lost sheep. We must be aware they
have been hurt and in their woundedness, they have
come to the church for healing. We must realize that
traditionally the church hasn't understood them, and
they have been left feeling rejected and isolated. Let
us not make the mistake of seeing only the surface
behavior and turning our backs on these children.
Let us not further alienate them from the true lifeline
in Jesus Christ, the church.

PEDIATRIC SPECIALISTS IN THE HOLY GHOST

The desire to see kids healed is what made me
begin to notice that wounded children often came
from single-parent homes. Their hurts were simply
deeper than those of the children who did not come
from single-parent homes, and, while the children
often didn't talk about their pain, it was intense and
caused them to act out in ways that had negative
repercussions for the rest of their lives. It was as
though they had been around Agent Orange, a defoli-

ation chemical used in the Vietnam War. Just as the effects of Agent Orange on many citizens and soldiers did not surface immediately, the effects of divorce do not show up quickly. Eventually, though, they rob the quality of peoples' lives.

I believe that in every wounded family there is gold. If the enemy has chosen to target them with a strategic hit, it is for a reason. Perhaps there is a Joseph, David, or Mary in the line, and Satan wants to destroy him or her. The church must not quit on them. As ministers of the gospel we must seek these souls with the same determination as we would the lost souls of the world, the least, and the lame. We cannot just write them off. Pediatric specialists in the Spirit are needed to bring the healing touch of Jesus to the children. The church needs men and women who have a lifetime call and commitment to youth ministry. We can no longer just provide a babysitter and call what we do youth ministry. From this day forth, let us provide children with youth pastors who take the responsibility for their young flock as seriously as any senior pastor takes responsibility for his adult charges. We must look with the compassionate eye of the pediatric specialist who can probe and find the woundedness in the child, and prescribe the proper medication. We want to see children grow and be transferred healthy and whole over the rough waters of adolescence. Like the pediatrician who diagnoses the physical problems of a wounded child and prescribes the necessary course of action, the church can, as pediatric specialists in the Holy Spirit, reach into the heart of the children and help them become healed.

BUILD A WALL OF FIRE

The church needs to challenge each of its members to check the foundational purpose according to which he or she lives, and to establish Christ as the glory and head of every heart and home. Living a life led by the power of Holy Spirit and keeping Jesus in the center of each household is the answer to Satan's attack on the home. This Spirit-led life is available to us individually and collectively. In the household of faith, we must see the importance of building a "wall of fire." As we have discussed, Zechariah spoke of God as the wall of fire that would protect Jerusalem. God said that He would be the glory in its midst (Zechariah 2:5). The fire of the Holy Ghost embodies the presence of the Lord. This holy fire will keep the enemy from attacking like a wolf from outside the perimeter of marriage, and it will keep those within the family safe and in love with one another. To build the wall of fire we must live with the awareness of the Holy Spirit in everything we do, asking ourselves in every situation, "What would Jesus do?" What a challenge! Knowing His will and living it in the home and in the secret places of our lives causes great spiritual heat to come upon the enemy, while bringing freedom for those that believe. Keep the fire stirred up; keep your will submitted to His. Stoke the fire with the fuel of obedience. *"My food,"* said Jesus, *"is to do the will of Him who sent me and to finish His work"* (John 4:34, NIV). Keep the fire crackling by continuing in the warmth of affection for one another.

THE WAR ZONE

Time and time again as I've traveled to minister to single-parent families, the fact that I have entered into a spiritual battle has become more apparent. And it is not just I who am under attack in this ministry. At seminars I often ask the single parents, "Who among you today had a difficult time in getting here?" Without fail, the majority raise their hands. It seems as if the path into this area of ministry, both to give it and to receive it, is lined with landmines. Countless obstacles arise to stop those who need to hear, as well as to hinder and discourage those who come to share the good news of restoration and forgiveness.

The Lord Jesus wants His church to gather those who have been caught in the crossfire of the attack on the marriage. There is wonderful educational material available to help stop the battle in the home — books on marriage and building strong families — and they are truly helpful, but they are not enough. The war isn't won until all the captives and casualties are brought home. If the church does not actively go after the wounded souls in the midst of the marriage break-up, there is the possibility of our losing the battle and, by our unwillingness to rescue them, allowing the enemy to continue to victimize the captives. I read some time ago of a downed U.S. military pilot, Scott O'Grady, whose airplane was shot down in the hills over Bosnia. The United States of America made an all-out effort to find and rescue this young man, mobilizing a billion dollars in rescue equipment and all the men and women needed to track and rescue their one downed comrade. They risked much for the life of one. In the war in the Spirit, can we do any less? We don't want generations to grow up behind enemy lines embittered, rejected, with deep feelings of abandonment because no one came to rescue them in the name of the Lord

Jesus. They may never come to the knowledge of Our Heavenly Father's love.

In the household of faith, we the church must boldly enter the field of battle declaring to the enemy, "We have been sent in Jesus' name to set the captives free." Those who are wounded and are being held captive are waiting to be set free.

As we enter the war zone, we need to be well prepared. Often, God's people are taken by surprise and are themselves ambushed. In these moments, the church must stay focused on the mission and remain faithful. The opportunities for victory are given to us, but not only must we stay on our knees, we need to be on our toes as well. We must stay in touch with God and also be alert to the tactics of the world, the flesh, and the devil. As the enemy tries to ambush us, let us strategize to ambush him, asking the Lord to send in his arrows to confuse him as God's word says in Psalm 144:6, *"Flash forth lightening and scatter them; Send out Thy arrows and confuse them."* We can become aware of set-ups and situations which cause us to fall into sin. The enemy is skilled in ambush but the Lord is better. The Lord is even able to turn the obstacles that the enemy sends our way into opportunities for His word to go forth.

We must prepare for the battle by interceding. Intercession is an essential weapon in single-parent ministry. My message to the church is "intercede to intercept Satan." He wants to keep God's children from receiving from the Father, and to keep people from ministering to the recipients. It seems that most people in leadership sense opposition as they move forward in this area of ministry. As I've minis-tered in Australia and New Zealand, the leaders of the host churches have come to realize that when ministry to the single-parent family begins, it's like entering a mine field of spiritual activity. Before doing a CHIPS weekend in which he was the liaison between CHIPS United States and CHIPS Australia, one elder in Australia said, "Tony, I have had the worst three months of my life." As one who ministers to single parent families, I've learned to proceed with great caution and not to take the strategies of the enemy lightly. He uses several types of landmines: sickness in the family, lack of finances, troubles with the house or car, difficulty with the kids, and general discouragement, especially during travel. There always seems to be some type of aggravation.

As I travel I am ever more aware of the need to walk closely with Jesus. The greatest area of frustration for me comes particularly in the area of airplane connections. My plans never seems to go smoothly. I experience obstacles either before I leave or during my travels. I sense the irritating, annoying presence of the enemy seeking to hinder the anointing. After many trials, I've learned the strategies and patterns of the enemy uses. Now as I enter the mine fields or sense the resistance, I praise the Lord for the Great Detector — the Holy Spirit. He has given me discernment to see what's going on. Now, as I prepare and travel, I see the enemy in every potential obstacle and am able to take him down before he can get in my face. I know God wants to show His love and to do something glorious in the midst of these distractions, so I've learned to praise Him for what he is *about* to do.

A single-parent seminar taught me much about the strategies of victory, our Father's great love for the single parent, and the great lengths to which He will go to free one captive. One autumn, early on a

Friday morning, I set out from my house in
Rochester, New York, on my way to Great Falls, Montana. I was scheduled to do a Single-Parent Day Seminar at a local church. The day was set up by an single parent who had heard me speak at a conference
and had requested her pastor invite me to Montana.
My flight was scheduled to leave Rochester Airport at
noon for Detroit and then connect to Minneapolis/St.
Paul. I was to change planes that night and fly to
Great Falls. I would arrive Friday night with plenty of
time for a Saturday morning start of the Single-Parent
Seminar.

At the crowded Detroit Metro airport I looked
out the window excited to be boarding what looked
to be a brand new 747. Amidst the noise of two hundred or more people, there was an announcement
that our flight had been canceled due to a worker
backing a luggage carrier into the plane, leaving a
hole in its side. We would have to catch another
flight three hours later. What had initially seemed like
an unchallenged plan of God had just suffered its first
ambush.

The second ambush was in the form of another non-working plane. I was seated on the plane, an
8:00 p.m. flight, when the announcement was made
that this plane could not fly due to a hydraulic brake
leak. This was after I had called the single parent
who had arranged for me to speak and reassured her
that I would make it to Montana on time.

At this point the only opportunity to get out of
Detroit was a 10:00 p.m. plane to Minneapolis. I
wanted to get out of Detroit and get as close to Montana as possible. However, I knew that for me to get
on the 10:00 p.m. plane would take divine intervention since there were now two planes that had been

grounded and a myriad of passengers looking for a way out. I searched to find someone who looked as though he was in charge and explained my dilemma. I showed him the brochure made up for the event with my picture on it. The Lord helped me to find favor in his eyes, and he said he would help. Miraculously, I got placed on standby level one, and through God's grace got on the 10:00 p.m. flight. I got into my seat, prayed, and thinking of Jonah confessing his sin to the sailors in the sinking boat, covered my head with a book so if anything went wrong the passengers would not point and shout, "It must be his fault!" All went well on this flight, and I arrived in my motel in Minneapolis/St. Paul at 1:00 a.m. Exhausted from the day, I went to sleep. I had no clean clothes, no toothpaste or toothbrush and neither did the airport hotel. My bags were somewhere on some plane, but I was grateful for a place to rest my head.

The next morning's flight to Montana was an early one. I awoke on time and arrived to find the plane waiting at the gate. I was a wrinkled mess but still optimistic that God was about to release blessing. The flight was on time, and the large plane was nearly empty, with only 7 people aboard. I was glad that I was on my way. With all that had transpired, my spirit was exceptionally excited with the anticipation of how the Holy Spirit would move in the meeting in Montana. After all the aggravation, I thought I had the situation all figured out. Something good was going to happen in Montana.

I sat in the first row behind the first class section reading my Bible. The Word was so alive to me on that beautiful morning that I couldn't write down the nuggets of gold being revealed to me quickly enough. As I read and the plane came to a cruising altitude, peanuts and beverages were handed out. Shortly following my peanut feast, I was interrupted by a flight attendant who came up to me and questioned, "Excuse me. Is that a Bible you're reading? Is there something going on in Great Falls? I couldn't help notice you reading, and there is a man in the rear of the plane reading a Bible also." I replied, "There's nothing going on that I know of outside of me holding a Single-Parent Day Seminar. It's a day of biblically-based teaching to single parents and children, presenting them with the message of wholeness through Jesus Christ." She asked, "Is that what you do? You're a minister? That's very interesting. I'm a single parent. Can I sit and talk with you?"

Flight attendants usually cannot afford the time to talk with all that they have to do, but this two hundred passenger plane had only 7 passengers. And so she sat and began to open up about her life to me. She told me that she had a little boy who was 18 months old and how much she loved him.

At this point, she lashed out at the little boy's father. She told me what a "creep" he was and how she hated him. I was aware of great venom in her heart, as the tirade continued for several minutes. As I listened, I felt the Holy Spirit's prompting me to share with her. When she finally stopped, I asked her if she loved her little boy. She answered, "Oh, he is the greatest little guy."

I asked her, "Would you want to do anything to hurt him?"

"No! No!" she said assuredly.

I truly felt the prompting of the Spirit to share some insights, so I began, "In my years of helping single parents and children I've found the biggest mistake single parents make with their children is holding bitterness and hatred in their hearts toward their children's other parent. The bitterness seems to pass on to the children, and eventually they rebel or take the side of the other parent. Children don't really want to take sides. They need the freedom to love both parents." I explained that many children grow up severely hampered due to parental strife.

She seemed startled and became very pensive. Her heart seemed to grow soft as she told me that she had once been a Christian and now had backslidden, and was drinking and living a sinful life. She said that her mother was a Christian who took her son to church each Sunday.

I asked her, "Don't you think it is time to turn to the Lord afresh?" I challenged her with the idea that the thing that was stopping her from returning to the Lord was all the hatred and bitterness in her heart. After some thirty minutes of uninterrupted conversation, I asked if she would feel comfortable in praying with me. She said "yes," and at 31,000 feet in the clouds I led her through a prayer asking the Lord for forgiveness for her sins and for the hatred held against her boy's father. Then she recommitted her life to Jesus Christ. Tears rolled down her face. She had all she could do to hold back the sobs. Her mascara dripped black lines down her cheeks. Glory be to God!

When I stopped she said in a very teary voice, "This is no accident; this plane is never this empty." Quickly I reflected on the events of the last 24 hours which led me to that moment, and I recounted some of them to her. I told her, "God loves you so much, and your soul is so valuable to Him that he put a hole in a brand new 37-million dollar aircraft just so that

you and I could talk!" We both rejoiced in His goodness. I told her that at her first chance, she should
call her mother and tell her that her prayers had been
answered. In leaving the plane, I got the nicest hug
I've ever gotten from a flight attendant, tears still in
her eyes. Praise God for the miracle at 31,000 feet.

Just as He reached out to help this flight attendant, our heavenly Father wants to help other single
parents, not condemn them. He will move mountains to reach them. As the church, let us be the car-
riers of the message that they should not hide from
Him, that they should run to Him.

THE FATHER'S ARMS EXTENDED

The Lord Himself in the person of the Holy
Spirit in us wants to be available to help people sort
out the difficulties that single-parent families experience. He wants to work through us. He can work
through the ending of the marriage and bring forth
life from the loss. I was in a meeting once when a
widow stood to testify. She said, "Tony, thank you
for the CHIPS ministry. I only wish it had been here
when I was raising my six children alone. There was
no one, but God." I wondered, "Why wasn't anyone
else there to help?" In my spirit, I asked the Lord,
"Lord, are you the only one that is supposed to help
these families? If so, I'll get out of your way." I
believe He responded to me with this thought, "Tony,
you can stop CHIPS now, but I will never stop reaching out to my wounded children. It is about time that
the body caught up with what the head has been
doing." God through Christ is the head of the His
body, the church, and we therefore must get in touch
with what the head has been and is doing.

I recall counseling a frightened little girl once, trying to employ my best pastoral counseling technique. Throughout our conversation I had said, "God loves you. Do you know that?" and "He has not given to you the spirit of fear but of power and love and a sound mind" and "God's love casts out all fear." She nodded her head and answered, "Yes, I know that God loves me, but sometimes I need Him to hug me!" So much for pastoral counseling! She was right. She does need God to hug her. Furthermore, God intends to hug her by means of the arms of His body on earth, you and me. In His Word, God says, *"I will not leave you as orphans. I will come to you"* (John 14:18).

Thus, there is a message here for the members of single-parent families as well as the members of the churches whom God wants to employ in meeting single-parent families' needs. Ironically, when both groups begin to hear the message, the message becomes the same for both: God wants to love His hurting children, without regard for their age or marital state, through His people. The only requirements are faith and obedience — the faith to believe that God loves you, that He can and will love others through you, and the willingness to obey His Word and His prompting concerning the expression of such love. Likewise, the Father wants to remove the mentality of brokenness in those that call upon His Son's name. He sent Him for the sake of the broken and crushed in spirit. In all homes, including the single-parent home, when Christ is lifted up as the head of the household, that family is not broken, but whole.

One way churches can participate in thwarting the enemy is to become a CHIPS "host church." A host church puts up the CHIPS banner and opens its doors once a month to minister to the needs of single-parent families. The CHIPS ministry helps train and equip the church to effectively reach out to the single-parent family. Even if a church does not wish to become a CHIPS host church, it can serve single-parent families by providing CHIPS resource materials to its single parent families.

For now, God has set CHIPS apart for a unique outreach to single-parent families. I believe, however, that the ministry will cease to be unique as the body of Christ comes to understand that it is God's will for the church — His body on earth — to conduct this ministry much as it already does to the poor or sick. The Lord is showing Himself through His Body as it reaches out to the individuals who need such ministry. The hurting people in single-parent families must be told of the love of God the Father, encouraged to face the sinfulness of their ways, receive forgiveness of sin through Christ His Son, and turn and be restored to the family and to fellowship by the power of the Holy Spirit. I know the church can make a difference as we follow the Father's heart. Consistent love and encouragement from the body of Christ helps to save those who have been wounded and targeted by the enemy. The single-parent family can find true life through Jesus Christ and live in wholeness.